Incorporating Social Goals
in the Classroom

of related interest

Asperger's Syndrome
A Guide for Parents and Professionals
Tony Attwood
ISBN 1 85302 577 1

Learning to Live with High Functioning Autism
A Parent's Guide for Professionals
Mike Stanton
ISBN 1 85302 915 7

Finding Out About Asperger Syndrome,
High-Functioning Autism and PDD
Gunilla Gerland
ISBN 1 85302 840 1

Asperger Syndrome, the Universe and Everything
Kenneth Hall
ISBN 1 85302 930 0

Blue Bottle Mystery
An Asperger Adventure
Kathy Hoopmann
ISBN 1 85302 978 5

Of Mice and Aliens
An Asperger Adventure
Kathy Hoopmann
ISBN 1 84310 00 7

Incorporating Social Goals in the Classroom

A Guide for Teachers and Parents of Children with High-Functioning Autism and Asperger Syndrome

Rebecca A. Moyes

Foreword by Susan J. Moreno

Jessica Kingsley Publishers
London and Philadelphia

The Teacher/staff skillstreaming checklist on pp.108–109, the Student skillstreaming checklist on p.110, the Parent skillstreaming checklist on p.111 and the Avoiding trouble table on p.139 are reproduced here with the kind permission of Research Press. The Observation profile on pp.113–117 is taken from Cumine, V., Leach, J. and Stevenson, V. (1998) *Asperger's Syndrome: A Practical Guide for Teachers*, London: David Fulton, and is reproduced with the kind permission of the publishers. The Accepts placement test on pp.118–119 is taken from the *Walker Social Skills Curriculum* (1998) and is reproduced with the kind permission of Pro-ed publishers. The Comic Strips Conversation on p.135 is taken from Gray, C. (1994) *Comic Strip Conversations*, Arlington, TX: Future Horizons, and is reproduced with the kind permission of the publisher. The preparation checklist for the IEP meeting on pp.162–163 is taken from Fouse, B. (1999) *Creating a Win-Win IEP for Students with Autism*, Arlington, TX: Future Horizons, and is reproduced with the kind permission of the publisher.

First published in the United Kingdom in 2001 by
Jessica Kingsley Publishers Ltd,
116 Pentonville Road, London
N1 9JB, England
and
325 Chestnut Street,
Philadelphia, PA 19106, USA.

www.jkp.com

Library of Congress Cataloging in Publication Data
A CIP catalog record for this book is available from the Library of Congress

British Library Cataloguing in Publication Data
A CIP catalogue record for this book is available from the British Library

ISBN 1 85302 967 X

Printed and Bound in Great Britain by
Athenaeum Press, Gateshead, Tyne and Wear

The world has only begun to experience your gifts and talents. You provide everyone who touches your life the treasure of your uniqueness and a chance to learn from it and appreciate it. If I could grant you one wish, it would be that you always find time to swim in your own ocean and be proud that God has made you such a special little boy.

I dedicate this book to my son, Chuckie.

Contents

Acknowledgements

Writing this book was probably the most daunting task I have ever attempted! These people deserve a special thank you for all their effort and support on my behalf:

- Susan J. Moreno of Maap Services for her dedication in keeping me positive and focused, and for being there when I needed her most.

- Dr. Joseph McAllister and Dr. Karleen Preator for believing in our son, committing themselves to making a difference in this field, and providing me with support whenever I have asked.

- Dr. Nancy Minshew for all her wonderful help over the years and also with her explanations of brain function for this book.

- Dr. Marilyn Hoyson for her assistance and for her special concern for our children.

- William Stillman for his sound advice and for making Pennsylvania families realize that 'the dreams that we dare to dream really do come true.'

- Diane Catterall, my special friend who assisted me tremendously with ABOARD.

- Carrie Buchanan, Phyllis Malone, Rebecca Volaire and Suzanne Zimmerman, for volunteering their time to help with the finer details of this book.

- Shirley Mumaw, my mother, for providing me with the gifts of compassion, kindness, understanding and who kept me writing by checking on my progress each day!

- William Mumaw, my father, for providing me with character, fortitude and the strength to see a job to the end.

- Cindy Martin, my sister and very best friend, and the aunt my children so adore.

- Skip Mumaw, my brother, and the most decent man I have ever known.

- 'Grandma', Richie, Freddie, Laurie, Lilly (and kids) for cheering me on when the going got tough!

- Kiersten, our beautiful, vibrant, and loving little girl who makes us laugh and see the world in a different light.

- To Chuckie, our son, who provided the reason and the purpose (and the computer expertise!).

- Charles Moyes, my husband, for putting up with printer noises, keyboard sounds, and fax signals at 2:00 a.m. for the last five years! His love is the foundation for everything I do, for all that I have become, and all that I will be.

- All the parents of children with autism who shared with me the many gifts of their stories, love for their children, and hope for their futures over the last several years. I thank you deeply and offer my prayers that your children may obtain all the goals you set for them.

- All children with autism for teaching me so many lessons I needed to learn. It is my sincere hope that this book will help their pathways be a little less hard to tread.

And most of all:

God in heaven, who gives me the strength to meet each day with courage, faith, and most of all, hope.

Foreword

As the parent of a young child with autism spectrum challenges, nothing riled me more than hearing 'pontifications' from some expert with a mile-long list of credentials who had never *done* what he or she was recommending! Now I am the parent of an adult who has attained much in her life, but still copes with those challenges. Even now, I still find it irritating to receive suggestions or instructions from someone who lacks practical experience. These same feelings are shared by the thousands of families with whom I have had contact in my work.

Rebecca Moyes can speak to us as someone with practical experience, both as a parent and educator.

I first had the pleasure of meeting Rebecca Moyes in her capacity as the director of a parent group in Pennsylvania. The founder of this group, Rebecca had taken it from a small gathering of parents to a large and powerful, statewide information and advocacy organization.

In her early adult years, Rebecca was a regular education teacher who often taught special needs children in her classroom. Later, she became the parent of two children, one of whom has Asperger's Syndrome. Rebecca has lived both sides of the special education service delivery system: parent and professional. In both capacities, she is caring, organized and highly effective.

I think you are in for quite a treat in reading this book and keeping it on hand as a reference. It is well-organized. The reader can locate a topic and study it briefly or deeply, according to available time and need. Most importantly for both parents and teachers, this book won't waste your time. Parents and professionals share a need for practical, rather than theoretical, advice. This book provides just that.

The book provides an excellent portrait of the social challenges involved in all disorders now found under the umbrella of autism spectrum disorders. However, the greatest strength of *Incorporating Social Goals in the Classroom* is its individualized education plan (IEP) and lesson-planning information. It is bursting with concrete examples of lesson plans and IEP goals. We all know that each child is an individual with unique needs. However, not all those who need to know how to write and/or request IEP goals and lesson plans have the creativity to read materials on the theory of these tasks and then come up with specific items to use in the classroom. That is what Rebecca's book accomplishes.

As I write this foreword, Rebecca's book is still several weeks from publication. I am already telling parents to be looking for it. I wish it were available right now, for the beginning of this school year. Happily, it will be in place by early spring so that parents and teachers can digest its content and then be fully prepared for the spring parent–teacher conferences from which most IEP's and lesson plans emerge.

I was so taken with the good, creative information in this book, that I have already asked Rebecca to present at my next International Conference on Individuals with Autism and Asperger's Syndrome. May Rebecca's book ease your educational burdens, as she has done for the fortunate families she has known since her child was diagnosed.

Susan J. Moreno, President and Founder, Maap Services;
Editor, The Maap; Parent

CHAPTER ONE

Is it Autism or Asperger Syndrome? – Diagnostic Criteria

In recent years, parents of children with high-functioning autism have been searching for a way to explain why their child has language, does not bang his/her head, and is able to participate in typical schools with relative success (for the most part) if they truly have 'autism.' They have learned that the label frightens and intimidates everyone they inform who must work with the child in some way (teachers, doctors, scout leaders, even relatives). Yet, they know there is a definite need to clarify with these individuals that their child has a problem so that he/she will not be misunderstood. They search for more appropriate explanations for their child's behavior and latch onto terms such as: sensory dysfunction disorder, auditory processing disorder, semantic pragmatic disorder, or social awareness disorder. They attach themselves to these labels because they don't quite feel 'at home' with the use of the word 'autistic,' and they don't want their child to be compared to individuals with this disorder who are silent and/or socially aloof.

Hans Asperger, a Viennese pediatrician, first described in 1944, (Asperger 1944) children who appeared to have autism but were more able in their use of language and in their social interactions. These children had fluent speech and a desire to interact with other children. They were intensely preoccupied with certain subjects, were poorly coordinated, had trouble with intricate social skills, and had little ability to empathize with others. He helped to initiate a treatment program for these children that included speech therapy, physical education, and drama practice to address these deficits.

Table 1.1 includes six categories of criteria (A – F) for the diagnosis of Asperger Syndrome, one of the pervasive developmental disorders.

Table 1.1: Diagnostic criteria for Asperger Syndrome from DSM IV (1994)

A. Qualitative impairment in social interaction, as manifested by at least two of the following:

1. marked impairment in the use of multiple nonverbal behaviors such as eye-to-eye gaze, facial expression, body postures, and gestures to regulate social interaction

2. failure to develop peer relationships appropriate to developmental level

3. lack of spontaneous seeking to share enjoyment, interests, or achievements with other people (e.g. by a lack of showing, bringing or pointing out objects of interest to other people)

4. lack of social or emotional reciprocity.

B. Restricted, repetitive, and stereotyped patterns of behavior, interests, and activities, as manifested by at least one of the following:

1. encompassing preoccupation with one or more stereotyped and restricted patterns of interest that is abnormal either in intensity or focus

2. apparently inflexible adherence to specific, nonfunctional routines or rituals

3. stereotyped and repetitive motor mannerisms (e.g. hand or finger flapping or twisting, or complex whole-body movements)

4. persistent preoccupation with parts or objects.

C. The disturbance causes clinically significant impairment in social, occupational, or other important areas of functioning.

D. There is no clinically significant general delay in language (e.g. single words used by age 2 years, communicative phrases used by age 3 years).

E. There is no clinically significant delay in cognitive development or in the development of age-appropriate self-help skills, adaptive behavior (other than in social interaction), and curiosity about the environment in childhood.

F. Criteria are not met for another specific Pervasive Developmental Disorder or Schizophrenia.

Reprinted with permission from the *Diagnostic and Statistical Manual of Mental Disorders*, 4th edn, copyright 1994 by the American Psychiatric Association.

Asperger Syndrome is diagnosed when a child has two social interaction impairments from the first category; one behavior pattern from the second category; a clinically significant impairment in social, occupational or other important area of functioning; no clinically significant general delay in language (e.g. single words used by age two, communicative phrases used by age three); no clinically significant delay in cognitive development or age-appropriate self-help skills or adaptive behavior; and when criteria are not met for another specific pervasive developmental disorder or schizophrenia.

The use of language is probably the most discriminating factor identifying these children with Asperger Syndrome, rather than high-functioning autism. However, it seems that today this disorder is being diagnosed far before the age when a child could demonstrate fluent speech! Thus, the explosion and overuse of this term has created much confusion among parents and educators.

The following questions and answers may help to clear up some of this confusion.

Is there a problem with using the wrong label?

For some children, yes! It becomes very difficult for certain children diagnosed after the age of five to qualify for services under the Individuals with Disabilities Education Act (IDEA) if their expressive language is considered normal and their academic abilities appear intact. In many states, before the age of beginning school attendance, a child is considered eligible for early intervention services for special education if he/she has a diagnosis of an autism/pervasive developmental disorder and has significant delays in areas that may affect his/her educational progress (speech/language, fine or gross motor skills, self-help skills, cognitive abilities). Children diagnosed with a pervasive developmental disorder at an early age generally do. However, if the child is diagnosed after the age of five, he/she must still demonstrate the need for specially designed instruction to be eligible to receive an individualized education plan (IEP). If this newly diagnosed child is *currently* able to make passing grades, control his/her behavior, exhibit age-appropriate fine and gross motor skills, and/or speak fluently, it becomes difficult to qualify for IEP services under IDEA for help with social skills. Special education personnel are becoming very aware of which labels require more services. The 'autism' label is generally considered to be a more severe label than 'Asperger Syndrome.' It is not a relief to a parent and of no help to the child diagnosed with a less severe pervasive developmental disorder if he/she can not obtain the necessary supports with this label. For this reason, it may be beneficial to use autism as the diagnosis rather than Asperger Syndrome.

Is there a way around the problem?

'Use the diagnosis that provides the services' (Attwood 1998, p.151). This author would like to add this warning: do not 'upgrade' an autism label to Asperger Syndrome when the child is transitioning from preschool to elementary school simply because the child is more able. The new label may exclude him/her from obtaining services in school districts more familiar with the diagnosis. For instance, in many elementary schools, language therapy is frequently not recommended for children who can speak, have age-appropriate pronunciation, and can understand the communication of others. However, language interventions can certainly include work on pragmatic language deficits (or the social, practical applications of language). Eliminating language therapy and language goals on the IEP because the child is fluent may have drastic repercussions for children with Asperger Syndrome later if pragmatic weaknesses are not addressed in another area of the child's IEP. For this reason, keeping the 'autism' label and the historical information about the child's development close at hand are recommended if he/she is in jeopardy of losing services.

What does 'high-functioning autism' refer to anyway?

The use of the term 'high-functioning' means that the child has average or above average intelligence. It has nothing to do with the number of autistic symptoms the child has. A child with 'high-functioning' autism could be a child who has many self-stimulatory behaviors, little social interactive ability, little expressive language, and yet has a near normal IQ score.

Can you sum it all up? Should we say it's Asperger Syndrome or high-functioning autism?

In this book, we will use both labels interchangeably. However, you should consider what the child needs in the way of services presently before determining which label you will use. Consider the child's prior history as a toddler. Include what services his/her doctors require for him/her to succeed now. Do not get hung up on choosing the most 'socially appropriate' label. Find descriptive literature that best describes the child to provide to educators and those working with him/her. Back this up with a doctor's evaluation and recommendations when you proceed to the IEP meeting to develop his/her educational 'map' for success.

What would you say is the greatest area of need for children with Asperger Syndrome or high-functioning autism?

Social skills instruction. Social skills instruction is by far the most misunderstood and least addressed area of need for children with Asperger Syndrome and high-functioning autism.

If teachers and professionals surveyed parents of children with Asperger Syndrome and/or high-functioning autism and asked them what their greatest desire is for their children, they may be surprised to discover that a good many of them would respond that they just want their children to have friends.

The ability to be accepted socially can be a huge predictor of a child's successfulness in later life. Their ability to obtain and keep a job in adulthood will largely be determined by their social adeptness. Parents of children with this diagnosis are much more aware of this than other parents. Children with Asperger Syndrome become very aware of their differences, often when they are as young as seven or eight years of age. This can cause poor self-esteem and even depression in many of these youngsters.

Many teenagers, when the demand for social interaction increases and becomes intricate and intense, will require medication to cope with their depression and anxiety. They will need a 'safe person' to turn to if they become targets for bullies and/or excessive teasing. They will need understanding teachers and parents who will be able to recognize if and when the 'mainstream' setting may not be working for them and be ready with modifications and adaptations. They will need, throughout their school years, a solid, age-appropriate social skills curriculum to help them address their inherent weaknesses in this area and enable them to meet with success not only in their school settings, but also in their homes and communities.

CHAPTER TWO

Deficits in Social Communication

'The school-age child spends as much of his time as possible in the company of his peers from whom he learns firsthand about social structure, about in-groups and out-groups, about leadership and followship, about justice and injustice, about loyalities and heroes and ideals...he learns the ways and standards of adult society.'

> – Joseph L. Stone and Joseph Church (1968) *Childhood and Adolescence: A Psychology of the Growing Person*

'Then you should say what you mean,' the March Hare went on.

'I do', Alice hastily replied, 'At least I mean what I say – That's the same thing you know.'

> – an excerpt from *Alice in Wonderland* by Lewis Carroll

The social weaknesses of children with high-functioning autism/ Asperger Syndrome can be grouped into two broad categories:

- deficits in social communication

- deficits in social behavior.

This chapter will address the deficits in social communication of children with this diagnosis and provide examples of how they might manifest themselves in the classroom.

Since many children with this diagnosis may have good expressive language, an excellent command of vocabulary, and age-appropriate pronunciation, educators may find that it is difficult to recommend them for language therapy. One speech therapist reveals the story of how she talked to nine-year-old Ian, a child with Asperger Syndrome, and asked him to describe to her what makes a friend. Ian replied, 'Someone who is in my class at school, is nine years old, a boy, and who has braces and short hair like mine.' Obviously, this illustrated to her that he had a strong grasp of the *use* of language, but that this child was in need of instruction in *social* language. He had adopted the belief that a friend was made up of physical parts because he was human. He completely missed the idea that a friend was someone to share secrets with, someone who had the same interests, someone who was there for you in times of need. Teaching children with high-functioning autism to label objects in language therapy and neglecting the social end of language will not help them to develop friendship-making skills. This type of instruction is called *pragmatics* ('in-practice' communication) and it provides us with the ability to have reciprocal social interaction with others.

o *Children with this diagnosis may have difficulty with turn-taking in conversation.*

Tony Attwood (Attwood 1998, p.13) describes a young girl who frequently baffled the postman with her uncanny ability to describe a particular type of diesel train. The postman could not interrupt her monologue and make an escape without being blunt. He marveled at her amazing knowledge of trains but was confused as to why she would think he needed to know all of this information. Dr. Attwood explains, 'A limited ability to have a reciprocal conversation is one of the core features of this syndrome.' Indeed, parents say that their children frequently interrupt and take over their conversations with their incessant questions or preoccupations.

○ *Children with Asperger Syndrome may have an intense interest in a particular subject and amass a huge store of knowledge about it. As adults, they may even become experts in their fields of interest. In conversation, they become preoccupied with chattering about their subject and fail to recognize that they may be boring or annoying their listener.*

EXAMPLE I

A ten-year-old with Asperger Syndrome is considered a 'computer expert.' He has read many adult computer manuals cover to cover and has memorized their contents. He is able to write programs, create web sites, and frequently trouble-shoots neighbors' and family members' computer problems. His parents, fully aware that some day this will be a wonderful career for him, are concerned that this intense preoccupation has not only limited his social time with peers, but also has isolated him because he monopolizes their conversations with talk of computers.

EXAMPLE II

Temple Grandin, a well-known adult woman with autism, describes her childhood passion with cattle and how it has created a successful full-time career for her in her adult years designing humane cattle-slaughtering facilities (Grandin 1995).

EXAMPLE III

One young man (who believes himself to be an undiagnosed adult with Asperger Syndrome) describes his passion for the Wizard of Oz. He has spoken on national television about his area of interest and is considered a foremost expert on the topic.

It should be explained that it isn't the interest in the topic itself that is the problem. It's the amount of time he/she devotes to this interest to the exclusion of everything else that a child of this age would normally be doing.

Frequently, when a young adult with Asperger Syndrome is taught to initiate a conversation with another peer, asking the other peer to describe his area of interest, the young person with Asperger Syndrome still manages to turn the conversation around to one of his favorite topics. This one-sided way of communicating can be quite annoying to typically developing young teens. Young girls, in particular, like to have the 'listening' ear of their friends to sympathize with their problems and concerns. One must be able to show concern and empathize with others at this age to be socially adept.

○ *Children with this diagnosis may use vocabulary that is 'odd.' They may use words that are far too advanced for their age. They may choose words because of their 'dictionary meaning' and not their 'conversation meaning.' Often, they are labeled 'little professors' because of their lecture-style conversation skills.*

EXAMPLE I

One preschool teacher excitedly told a parent of a four-year-old recently diagnosed with Asperger Syndrome disorder how remarkable her child was and explained that he couldn't possibly have a disability. She relayed happily how he replied to her query at snack time, 'Would you like some juice?' She was quite astounded when the child examined his cup and then clearly replied, 'Yes, perhaps I would.'

EXAMPLE II

A nine-year old girl with Asperger Syndrome was riding home in her parent's car with another friend after a Girl Scout meeting. The girl with Asperger Syndrome was talking incessantly about her favorite video game and finally her friend remarked, 'Why do you always use such big words?' The girl with Asperger Syndrome replied, 'If you perused the dictionary like I do, maybe you could use big words as well.'

EXAMPLE III

A ten-year old boy with high-functioning autism thoroughly enjoyed his dinner of roast beef and asked his mother if he could have some more 'game.' It took several minutes before his mother understood what he was referring to.

Children with this disorder may also 'invent' words or use them inappropriately. For instance, Tony Attwood (Attwood 1998, p.82) writes that one little boy whose room was messy reported to his parents that he was 'tidying down' (instead of 'tidying up') his room. Another girl described her ankle as the 'wrist of my foot.'

o ***Some children with high-functioning autism or Asperger Syndrome are very literal in their understanding of spoken language.***

There are frequently no gray areas for these children. Black is black, white is white, rules are rules. It becomes difficult for them to understand, for instance, why 'lying' is wrong but why 'white lies' are sometimes acceptable. Teachers frequently report that these are the children that obey school rules at all costs, and also report others to them who are not.

EXAMPLE I

One young boy with Asperger Syndrome got into trouble when playing outside during recess. He was throwing pebbles, and the teacher asked him to stop. He immediately referred to the rule chart and said, 'Throwing stones is not listed on the chart.' He was sent in to complete recess in a time-out room for being disrespectful. His parents had to explain to the teacher that he had memorized the rules on the chart and didn't realize there were more. They also had to explain to their son that it is impossible to mention all the rules on such a small chart and that some of the rules have to be 'assumed' by the students.

EXAMPLE II
A family was attending a local school football game with their child with Asperger Syndrome. They were directed by a police officer to park in a 'No Parking Zone' (marked by a 'No Parking' sign). The child with Asperger Syndrome refused to get out of the car because he believed they were 'breaking the law' by parking in the 'No Parking Zone.' It took much explanation to convince him that the police officer would not let them park there if it wasn't okay.

EXAMPLE III
One mother shares this story: 'When I tell my son to wipe his shoes before coming into the house, he frequently bends down and wipes them with his hands.'

EXAMPLE IV
Staff at a group home provide the residents with clean sheets each Wednesday and instruct them to 'change their beds.' They were baffled that a young man with autism would move his bed each Wednesday but would not change his sheets. Finally they realized that he was doing *exactly* what was instructed – changing his bed.

EXAMPLE V
A kindergarten teacher instructed the students to remove their shoes because they were getting her circle-time mat dirty. A student with Asperger Syndrome refused to do this and created quite a scene when she tried to remove them herself. He began to shout, 'I see London, I see France!' His mother had taught him that when his underclothes show,

children may tease him by chanting this rhyme. He equated his socks with his underclothes.

EXAMPLE VI

Liane Holliday Willey (Willey 1999, p.23) writes that her first-year teacher in school instructed her to 'find her mat and take a nap.' Liane refused to comply on several occasions. Finally her parents were called in. When her mother asked why she would not take a nap on her mat, Liane replied, 'I do not have a mat.' 'You most certainly do! It is in your cubby!' her teacher said smugly. Liane then stated: 'That is not a mat, it is a rug!' From then on, she would comply when the teacher instructed her to 'find her rug and take a nap.'

This literal interpretation of the language, as we have now seen, can create quite a disturbance in understanding communication in both the school and home arenas. Parents and educators need to be on the look-out for such times when a student is viewed as non-compliant and when he/she is insistent on doing things a certain way. It may appear to them that the child is perfectly intelligent and should quite easily be able to make the 'jump' from memorizing a rule to applying it. However, this is one of the core deficits of children with this disorder. Noncompliance may simply be the result of his/her very literal interpretation of directions, rules, or things that he/she has applied as 'the truth according to me.' This certainly is frustrating to these children who are trying to make sense of the world and learn proper social behavior by memorizing rules. They then have to turn around and learn that there is usually an exception to every rule!

○ *A common feature of children with Asperger Syndrome is that they may lack voice inflection in conversation, sometimes referred to as 'prosody.' They may speak at one pitch level – sometimes very high or very low. Those children who have voice inflection often sound 'rehearsed.'*

The speech of children with Asperger Syndrome may lack variation. Dr. Nancy Minshew reports that the melodic line of speech is produced by variations in pitch, rhythm, and stress. Prosody enables us to understand the 'changes in stress on compound words which may or may not change their meaning ("green house" and "greenhouse" or "uphill work" versus "walking uphill")' (Minshew, 1988, p.591).

Children with autism may take on a monotonous, one-pitch type of rhythm. Some educators refer to this type of prosody as 'robotic.' A mother reported recently that her son's voice has a 'twang' as if he was born in the southern part of the United States, even though they have always resided in Pennsylvania. Some parents report that their children can not adjust the volume of their voice, even when prompted to 'speak up' or 'talk quietly.' Children with Asperger Syndrome may also speak very quickly, especially when agitated, making it difficult to follow their train of thought.

EXAMPLE I
One young girl with Asperger Syndrome adopted the voice of the 'Big Bird' Sesame Street character. Her accuracy of this voice imitation was uncanny. It quickly became annoying to adults who frequently encouraged her to use her own voice. However, when she reverted back to her own voice, she spoke very quietly and with a flat tone.

○ *Individuals with this disorder may also have difficulty recognizing the use of irony or figures of speech in conversation.*

As previously discussed, the very literal interpretation of language may prevent these individuals from understanding idioms such as 'put a lid on it' or 'step on it' or 'the early bird gets the worm.' They may very well have to be taught these phrases and their meanings rotely.

EXAMPLE I
A mother was preparing to take her daughter with Asperger Syndrome to a baby shower. The girl put on her raincoat, even though the day was sunny and went out to the car. Her mother asked her why she was wearing a raincoat. She replied that she didn't want to get wet at the shower.

o *Individuals with this disorder may also experience difficulty with sarcasm.*

Because of their literal interpretation of the language, it may be too hard for them to decipher the real meaning behind the words. For instance the phrase 'Oh great!' which is sometimes used to express frustration, may not be interpreted correctly by a child with Asperger Syndrome.

EXAMPLE I
A nine-year-old boy with this disorder was instructed to go to the blackboard in school and write the multiplication product for 9 × 9. When he could not comply, the instructor said with sarcasm (and quite inappropriately), 'Some time today would be nice, Michael.' Later that day, during reading time, Michael completely surprised the class when he went to the board and wrote '81.'

o *Children with Asperger Syndrome may be accused of being too blunt with their friends and peers, and also with adults.*

Parents often joke that if you want the truth, ask an individual with Asperger Syndrome. Their strong sense of what is right and wrong may make it impossible for them to tell a lie. Teachers may find that these are the 'tattle-tale' children who are frequently willing to point the finger of accusation at their classmates for wrongdoings.

This quality does not endear them to their peers. Consider this example:

EXAMPLE I
A teacher instructed her class to pass their handwriting sample to the student beside them for this student to grade. The students were told to circle anything that did not look neat, was below or above the line of handwriting, or was too light or too dark. When a boy with Asperger Syndrome received his neighbor's work, he immediately began making many circles on the student's paper. When the paper was returned to his neighbor, his neighbor became angry and demanded to know why he had marked so many things wrong with his work. The boy with Asperger Syndrome replied, 'It doesn't look like the book!'

EXAMPLE II
A typical ten-year-old boy confided to a child of the same age with Asperger Syndrome at a science show that he was worried that his science project was not good enough. The boy with Asperger Syndrome replied, 'Don't worry about it; everyone else did the same experiment this year too. If it doesn't work, they can just look at someone else's.'

o *These children may find it difficult to focus on two things at once, often referred to as 'joint focus of attention.' This can affect their use of social language.*

EXAMPLE I
Six-year-old Emily, a child with Asperger Syndrome, was coloring a picture of flowers intently. Her mother asked, 'Emily, would you like a snack?' Emily did not reply. Her mother asked her again. Emily still did not reply. Finally, when Emily had finished coloring a flower, her mother asked again. This time, Emily replied, 'Yes.'

○ *Children with Asperger Syndrome may have difficulty judging proper body distance when communicating with another person.*

Teachers and parents frequently report to us that individuals with this diagnosis do not seem to be aware of where their bodies are in space, and what may be acceptable and unacceptable in conversation with regards to this matter.

EXAMPLE I
Sherry, the mother of a teenage boy with Asperger Syndrome, says that her son frequently makes people uncomfortable when he speaks. He positions himself too closely to the other individual and invades their 'space.'

Another common feature of the language of children with high-functioning autism or Asperger Syndrome is pronoun reversal (for example, they may say 'you' when they mean 'I'). For instance, a child may comment to an adult, 'You want a cookie' instead of, 'I want a cookie.' They may also refer to themselves in the third person or use their own name instead of the word 'I.'

The use of *echolalia,* the immediate or delayed repetition of the speech of others, often without regard to the meanings of their utterances, is also a common feature in the language of children with high-functioning autism or Asperger Syndrome. Dr. Barry Prizant has devoted much study to children with autism and their use of echolalia. He estimates that 85% of children with this disorder who have acquired speech have used echolalia (Prizant 1987). For this reason, parents and teachers should be careful that they are not trying to extinguish echolalia without careful consideration of its communicative intent. For instance, if a child is using echolalia to calm herself, forcing her to extinguish it may only serve to increase her stress.

After studying videotapes of over a thousand utterances of four children with autism, Prizant presents that immediate echolalia can be grouped into seven functional categories (Prizant and Duchan 1981). These categories are:

1. Turn-taking (turn fillers in a verbal exchange)

2. Declarative (labels objects, actions, or location)

3. Yes-answer (indicates affirmation)

4. Request (requests objects or others' actions)

5. Nonfocused (no apparent intent; often produced in states of high arousal)

6. Rehearsal (a processing aid; followed by utterance or action)

7. Self-regulatory (used to regulate one's own actions).

EXAMPLE I: TURN-TAKING
A teacher asked a child with autism, 'Are you going to the carnival tonight?' The child looked up, but did not answer. The teacher said, 'I'll bet you'll ride the merry-go-round.' The child responded, 'Ride the merry-go-round.' In this instance, the child was attempting to converse with the teacher and take his turn in conversation.

EXAMPLE II: DECLARATIVE
A preschool child with Asperger Syndrome was looking at a book of animals. Frequently, her mom would review the animals in the book and the appropriate sounds they made with the child. The child pointed to a cow and said to herself out loud, 'What does the cow say?'

EXAMPLE III: YES-ANSWER
A kindergarten teacher was passing out juice during snack time. She asked a child with Asperger Syndrome: 'Do you want some juice?' The child

replied, 'Do you want some juice?' The child was answering in the affirmative. The teacher can model the correct answer to him by saying, 'Yes! I want some juice!' but still respond to his attempt to communicate his desire for juice.

EXAMPLE IV: REQUESTS OBJECTS OR ACTIONS
Frequently, a first-grader with autism would approach the teacher and ask, 'You want Thomas?' 'You want Thomas?' He was asking his teacher to get the 'Thomas the Train' video for him.

EXAMPLE V: NON FOCUSED
A teacher shares that one boy in her classroom would sometimes comment, 'What goes around comes around' when the students were quiet or completing worksheets.

EXAMPLE VI: REHEARSAL
Frequently, when leaving preschool, a parent of a child with Asperger Syndrome would prompt the child to say goodbye to his teacher. She would instruct him using the phrase, 'Say Goodbye, Matthew!' Often Matthew would respond, 'Say Goodbye!' when leaving the classroom.

EXAMPLE VII: SELF-REGULATORY
Another young child with Asperger Syndrome was quite agitated over a change in his schedule. He began to pace the floor with a worried expression declaring, 'All done! Time for lunch!' using the exact words his teacher uses when art activities are done and lunch is about to begin. He was using this form of echolalia as a means of self-regulation to manage stress. His teacher can help ease his anxiety next time by providing him with advanced warning of transitions. As another example, one can also recall the script from the movie *Rain Man* where Raymond calms himself before entering a new hotel by chanting a comedy routine from *Abbott and Costello.*

Echolalia is more likely to occur under specific environmental and interactional conditions (Quill 1998, p.113), including:

- when a child is asked to participate in challenging activities
- during stressful times
- during unstructured times
- during transitions
- when the child is having difficulty processing the language.

There are several intervention strategies recommended for echolalia (Quill 1998, pp.119–122):

- Prepare for transitions that may cause stress for the child, use visual cues to prompt the child through the transition.
- Eliminate unstructured time.
- Watch for sensory overload.
- Simplify language input (do not exceed the child's comprehension abilities).
- Change the interaction style (eliminate 'wh' questions, use prompts, allow enough processing time).
- Model correct responses for the child.

The ability to participate successfully in social conversation is an art. Some of us are born with more tools than others to negotiate the fine nuances that make us an expert in this area. The skills that make us successful communicators can be taught and rehearsed so that we are not as awkward with them. Educators and parents need to realize that children with this disorder are every bit as hampered with this disability as children with physical disabilities. Their future lives are at stake: being able to complete advanced education;

interview and obtain jobs; work successfully with fellow employ-ees; date and marry. These milestones of our lives are all dependent upon the ability to have solid communication skills. An IEP that does not address communication and language issues cannot be considered an appropriate education for children with this dis-order.

LESSON PLANS

Lesson plan 1

IEP goal
Student will be able to demonstrate turn-taking and maintaining the subject of conversation with peers.

Materials needed

- 'Conversation Starter' cards, enough for half of the children in the group.
- Paper and pencils, enough for half of the children in the group.

Introduction
When we speak to our friends or classmates, we should always try to take turns. First one person speaks and then another. The person who is not speaking needs to listen. The person who is speaking needs to let the other person have a chance to speak too. People like to have con-versations with people who let them talk about the things they enjoy. When you speak with someone, you should talk about things that the other person enjoys as well. You should try not to change the subject and talk about something different if *both* of you have not finished the

first subject. Today we are going to practice taking turns in conversation and sticking to one subject.

Student practice

We are now going to play a little game called 'Finish the Story.' We will begin with one of you, and each of you will get a chance to contribute, one at a time. I will start off a story, and ask one of you to make up the next part, sticking to the main idea. Then, it will be someone else's turn to add a part, when I call on you. You must listen to the person who goes ahead of you so that your part fits with the story. You should not speak unless it is your turn. Ready?

'Today, I counted all the money I had saved from birthdays and allowances. It came to $30. I wanted my mom to take me to the toy store to see what I could buy. She agreed to do it after I ate my lunch. After lunch, we drove to the store. When we walked in the door…'

(Call on a student to continue the story, and then call on other children at random to keep the story going. Prompt each child to stick to the subject matter at hand. If they wander from the subject, they must think of a sentence or two that fits with the theme. Praise them if they do. Have all the children in the group contribute.)

Additional student practice

Now, we are going to break into pairs. I'm going to give each pair a 'Conversation Starter' card. One of you should read the 'Conversation Starter' card to the other person. That person will then reply to the question on the card. Then the other person will reply, etc. Each of you should have at least five replies back and forth for a total of ten replies. The person who has the 'Conversation Starter' card should keep track of the number of replies. When you reach ten replies, trade your card with another group's card. Then have your partner start the conversation with the 'Conversation Starter' card and keep track of the ten replies with this card. (Pass out 'Conversation Starter Cards.' These cards may say, for example, 'I really enjoy collecting Pokemon cards, do you?' or 'My favorite music group is the Backstreet Boys. What's yours?').

Additional practice for the student with Asperger Syndrome

(At this time, the students, still in pairs, can begin a conversation of their own, using their own topic of discussion. One of the students in the pair should begin a conversation. There must be five exchanges from each person: ten in total. On the eleventh exchange, the person may change the subject. This new exchange counts as one. Then, there must be five exchanges from each person about that subject. On the eleventh exchange, the topic of discussion can again be changed, beginning a new cycle. This allows each student in the pair to be able to change the subject and initiate a new conversation after ten exchanges. Later, after completion of this lesson, the teacher may encourage one or two peers to prompt the child with Asperger Syndrome when he/she is not sticking to the topic of conversation, or not making exchanges appropriately. Coaching these peers on what to say to the child with Asperger Syndrome would be useful: 'Johnny, we aren't talking about trains now. We are talking about Pokemon cards. Do you have any Pokemon cards?')

Parental practice

At home, parents should prompt the child when he/she is trying to change the topic of conversation or not taking turns. Parents can practice this same exercise, explaining its importance to the student. At times, keeping track on paper of how many appropriate exchanges were made will be useful to the student so that he/she can visually 'see' his/her improvement in this area. Parents can also 'listen in' on play dates with children in the home. By writing the topic of conversation down and how many appropriate exchanges were made, they can easily test for mastery of the goal.

Lesson plan 2

In Chapter 6, the use of Carol Gray's 'social stories' (Gray 1994) to teach social behavior is explained. This lesson contains a social story written to address the student's problem with being too literal.

IEP goal

The student will be able to demonstrate an understanding of words with multiple meanings.

Materials needed

- Paper and pencil.
- Three-ring binder.

Introduction

Sometimes when people say things, we get confused because words may have two or more meanings, and we only know one of those meanings. For instance, when someone says to you, 'step on it!' you may think that you should actually take your foot and step on something. However, 'step on it!' may actually mean, 'hurry up!'. Here is a story that may help you understand what I mean:

Words That Have More Than One Meaning

Sometimes I think that I am following directions.

I listen to what the speaker says to do, and I do just that.

Then, I find that I am doing the wrong thing.

This sometimes makes me upset.

When this happens, I will try to play the words over in my head and think of another meaning those words could have.

If I don't know the other meaning, I will ask the speaker to explain it again without getting upset.

I will tell the speaker I do not understand.

Most people are willing to explain things again for me if I ask.

I know the problem will be resolved if I am patient.

Student practice

(The student should read the story with the teacher and discuss its meaning.)

Additional practice for the student with Asperger Syndrome

(At this point, it may be useful to use the paper and pencil and write down some other idioms or metaphors that the student may hear such as 'pulling my leg', 'get a move on it,' 'changing your mind.' The teacher should write these in one column. Beside that column, the teacher and student should discuss each of their meanings and write these down. The student should also be encouraged to think up some of his/her own. From time to time, the teacher can quiz the student on the meanings of the idioms and metaphors.)

Parental practice

The idea above can be expanded and the papers kept in a three-ring binder notebook and referred to often. When additional ones are stumbled upon, these, too, can be added to the booklet. This is a very rote way of teaching children with Asperger Syndrome to be less literal. The student can use his/her excellent memory to help recognize and recall these interpretations when they occur in conversation in the future.

Lesson plan 3

Chapter 6 discusses the use of drama in helping to teach social skills. This lesson will use drama to teach students with Asperger Syndrome about using expression in their voices and some ideas suggested by Tony Attwood (Attwood 1998).

IEP goal

The student will be able to demonstrate proper voice inflection in conversation.

Materials needed

- Children's short stories, age-appropriate.
- Word cards, enough for half of the students.

Introduction

Boys and girls, it is important that when we talk to other people, we use our voices as well as our words to help get our message across. For instance, if I was angry, I might read the following message to you in this way (demonstrating controlled anger):

> 'I am upset because you left the lid off of the paint can, and it is all dried up.'

If I am really angry, I might say it the following way (read above sentence again and demonstrate much anger).

Depending on how we emphasize our voices, we can change the meanings of sentences. (Write the following sentence on the board:)

> 'I did not take the last candy bar out of the dish.'

Student practice

If we read the sentence and emphasize the first word, 'I', we are stating that 'I' didn't take the candy bar, somebody else did.

Can someone read the sentence and emphasize the word 'not' for us? (A student reads.) How does this make the meaning of the sentence different than when we emphasized the word 'I'? (The students should be called upon to read the sentence again, each time emphasizing different words: 'take,' 'last,' 'candy bar,' 'out,' 'dish.' Discuss with the students how the meaning of sentences have changed each time.)

Additional student practice

(Next, each student is given a card with one of the following expression words written on it:

happy	**tired**	**babyish**
sad	**afraid**	**complaining**
excited	**soft**	**bored**
angry	**loud**	**disappointed**

They then must say the days of the week with a paper in front of their face using the expression of the word on their card. The other children should try to guess the expression they are conveying by the sound of their voice.)

To add interest in our conversation and encourage people to want to listen to us, we should emphasize some words in our conversation. When we talk like a robot, people do not like to listen to us very long. I'm going to ask you to take turns reading the various parts of a story-book play. You should try to put as much emphasis into the parts as you can. (Teacher begins having each child read a few lines, coaching them to display emotion and read the part with 'feeling.' He/she should try to select the child with Asperger Syndrome to participate.)

Parental practice

The teacher should encourage the parents to have their child practice reading with expression and speaking with expression. This can be accomplished by selecting materials from newspapers, favorite books, or comics. The parent can read to the child using a particular expression, and the student can read back using the same expression.

Lesson plan 4

As outlined in Chapter 6, the use of videotape can be an excellent way to introduce or reinforce a social skill.

IEP goal

The student will refrain from being blunt or rude with peers.

Materials needed

- Red-light, green-light laminated cards (see Figure 2.1 on page 43).

- Videotape of inappropriate conversational behavior that is age-appropriate. (Oscar the Grouch from Sesame Street, Lucy from Charlie Brown, Angelica from Rugrats, and some of the Looney Tune characters are all classic examples of characters that demonstrate blunt or rude behavior.)

- 'Situation' cards, enough for every other student.

Introduction

When we say things that hurt our friends' feelings, or when we say things in an angry voice, it makes them feel as if they do not want to be our friends anymore. Being 'blunt' or 'rude' are the terms we use to describe this type of behavior. Let's watch this videotape. We will then talk about some inappropriate behaviors.

Student practice

(Students watch tape. Teacher then guides students through discussion, pointing out parts of the tape that demonstrated blunt or rude conversation.)

Additional student practice

(Divide the students into pairs. Give one student in each pair a situation card. The student should read the card to his/her peer, and the peer will then respond with an appropriate comment. For instance, one card could read, 'Pretend that I just got a new hair cut. It is way too short. I hate it, and I am very embarrassed. I ask you, "What do you think about my new hair cut?"' The peer should respond with a comment that is not blunt or rude. The class should listen to each response and evaluate whether or not they are appropriate. The cards can then be traded so that the other peer in each pair can practice.)

Additional practice for the student with Asperger Syndrome

(The teacher can explain to the student that when she observes appropriate conversation with peers, she will discreetly give him a 'green-light' laminated card. Green traffic lights mean 'Go! You are doing a great job!'. When the student may not be exhibiting appropriate conversation with a peer, the teacher may give him a 'red-light' card. Red traffic lights mean 'Stop!' Instruct the student that if he receives a red-light card and does not know what he was doing wrong, he should ask the teacher. She will either privately explain it at that moment or tell him when she will have time to explain it. If he does know what he has done wrong, he should try to apologize and discontinue the behavior.)

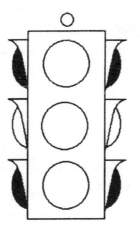

Figure 2.1

Parental practice

The red-light cards and green-light cards should be sent home with the student at the end of the day. The parents should review with the teacher and with the student what happened at school and reinforce the problem areas for the student. The parents could also keep a chart of how many green-light cards the student receives for a week and devise a reward.

Lesson plan 5

IEP goal
The student will be able to demonstrate joint focus of attention in conversation with another peer.

Materials needed

- Reading material, age-appropriate to the student.
- Pieces of clay.

Introduction
Sometimes it is necessary for us to be able to do two things at once. We need to be able to train our brains to attend to several things at one time so that we don't become overloaded and shut down. Otherwise, we may miss important instructions in school or have difficulty talking with friends. We are going to practice paying attention to two things at one time.

Student practice
First, we will practice reading a story by itself.
    (Have the student read a story.)

Next, we will practice making a skinny snake out of clay.
    (Have the student make a snake.)

Now, let's see if you can read the story and make the snake at the same time!
    (Have the student complete this task.)

Additional student practice

What is your favorite fairy tale? (Student should be able to describe a fairy tale in enough detail that the teacher knows he/she can recall it.) Now we are going to have you make a ball out of the clay and tell me that story at the same time. Can you do it? (Student should proceed.)

Parental practice

The parents should practice joint focus of attention activities with the child several times a week. Children can be encouraged to complete such activities while watching TV or at other times when it appears the child is difficult to distract.

Lesson plan 6

IEP goal

The student will demonstrate the ability to use proper body distance when speaking with another individual.

Materials needed

• Six-foot piece of yarn, smaller pieces of yarn.

(The song *Personal Space Invader* by Jeannie Tyons played before this lesson, would help set a light tone to the activity.)

Introduction

When people talk, they should stand a certain distance away from each other. Everybody has an amount of space around them that is called their 'personal space.' Personal space should not be intruded on by other people because it makes us feel uncomfortable. When someone stands too close to us, it makes us want to step back from them. We aren't able to listen to what they are saying because we feel uncomfortable because the other person is too close to us. (Demonstrate what too close is like.)

There is a good way to measure personal space and this is by using the 'three-foot' rule. Imagine that you could draw an invisible circle all the way around your body that was three feet away (demonstrate this with your arms for a visual prompt). This would be your personal space. You should not go into another person's personal space when you are speaking to them. Sometimes, however, when you need to tell a secret, or when you want to give someone a kiss or a hug, it becomes necessary to break this rule and move into their personal space. Sometimes you may have to sit or stand very close to someone because of circumstances, like a crowded elevator or a church pew. You will notice that everyone else is in the same position because of this circumstance, and you do not need to worry about the three-foot rule. However, *usually* when you are talking to your friends or grown-ups, you will need three feet of space between you and the other person.

Student practice

(Tie a piece of yarn around the student's waist, with a three-foot 'tail' remaining. Holding the 'tail' in front of the child, the teacher should demonstrate that this is the amount of personal space that everyone needs when they talk to another person. Next, make the tail smaller to demonstrate an acceptable amount of personal space when people are telling secrets or talking privately.)

Additional student practice

From now on, when I see that you may be standing too close to someone, I may give you a piece of yarn to help you remember. This will be our special signal that no one else will know, except for you and me and your parents. When you get a piece of yarn from me, you will know that you need to move two steps backwards from the other person because you are too close to them. You can then throw the yarn away or put it in your pocket.

Parental practice

Parents can continue prompting their child at home with pieces of yarn as described above.

CHAPTER THREE

Deficits in Social Behavior

'Come along in then, little girl!
Or else stay out!
But in the open door she stands
And bites her lips and twists her hands
And stares upon me trouble-eyed:
'Mother,' she says, 'I can't decide!
I can't decide!'

— Edna St. Vincent Millay

As we mentioned in Chapter 2, the social weaknesses of children with high-functioning autism/Asperger Syndrome can be grouped into two broad categories:

- deficits in social communication

- deficits in social behavior.

This chapter will address the deficits in social behavior of children with this diagnosis.

○ *Children with this diagnosis may display a weakness in perspective-taking ability; they have trouble 'stepping into another person's shoes.' They may also have trouble being able to practice introspection of their own behavior.*

One can see very quickly how this can be a problem when children with this diagnosis have trouble showing empathy or understanding towards others. They may also not understand if their own feelings of anger or frustration are justified. They have difficulty separating these intense feelings from the situation, evaluating whether their reactions are appropriate, and what may be triggering them. Although they may be able to recognize when others are angry or upset with them, they may have trouble deciphering what their part was, if any, in causing this anger.

EXAMPLE I

A sixth-grade student with Asperger Syndrome was put in the awkward position of having to 'grade' another student's throwing ability in gym class using a point scale. If a student threw a ball and hit the bull's eye, he was given 3 points. If he missed the bull's eye, he was given 1 point. The child with Asperger Syndrome graded the student with a '1,' as he very literally applied the directions the gym teacher had provided for hitting a target with a throw. The Asperger Syndrome child explained that the other child had hit the *edge* of the bull's eye with several throws, but the ball *had not actually entered* the bull's eye, thus earning a score of '1' and not '3'. The child with Asperger Syndrome could not understand why the other student was angry with him.

EXAMPLE II

One young man with Asperger Syndrome entered a hospital room to visit a sick uncle with his parents. He immediately approached his cousin (the hospitalized uncle's son) and began telling him his favorite joke, oblivious to the fact that the cousin was consumed with worry about his father.

o *Young children with this diagnosis may have trouble with imitation skills and pretend play; that is, they may not know how to engage in pretend play, may be rigid with the rules of the play, or they may withdraw for unacceptable time periods into pretend play.*

Frequently parents of young children with autism say that they never see their children 'playing house' or 'playing dress-up'. These are crucial activities in the development of social skills because as Kathleen Quill states (Quill 1995, p.200): 'the transition from simple to advanced pretense is a major turning point in the play development of children with autism. Failure to imagine and achieve insight into the perspectives of others has extreme consequences for a person's ability to make sense of the world.'

EXAMPLE I
Donna Williams (Williams 1992, p.39), a woman with high-functioning autism, reports that in her younger years, she was given a doll carriage. However, she had no idea what to do with it. She comments that she would frequently bang the carriage up and down the steps, certainly not playing with it in its intended way. She pushed it and pulled it, but did not understand the pram was to be used for taking her dolls for a 'walk.'

EXAMPLE II
Liane Holliday Willey (Willey 1999, p.18) writes that she frequently liked to create elaborate table settings out of tin foil to serve as plates, cups, silverware, serving platters, even food to play tea party with her imaginary friends. Interestingly, she remembers making the things a tea party would need, but not actually playing tea party. She would become angry when her playmates came to visit and when they rearranged or wanted to actually use the things that she had carefully created.

EXAMPLE III
A ten-year-old boy with Asperger Syndrome has a variety of stuffed animals which he keeps on his bed. He calls them his 'friends.' His mother says that after school, her son plays with his 'friends' until supper,

engaging in elaborate make-believe activities to the exclusion of everything else. He would continue this activity until bedtime if allowed.

There is a kind of hierarchy that exists for the social dimension of play (Parten 1932). This hierarchy suggests that a typical child moves from isolated play, where he/she appears to be unaware of others and occupies him/herself with only momentary interest in activities or materials, to a more oriented type of play where he/she has a better awareness of other children. In this first stage, the child shows an interest in other children, but does not attempt to enter into play with them. Next, the child moves on to a more parallel/proximity type of play where he plays beside rather than with other children. They may share toys or space with other peers, there may be some occasional interaction, but for the most part, it is still independent play. Later, the common-focus type of play where a child directly engages in turn-taking, gives and receives assistance and directives, and shares materials begins to emerge. There is also a common focus of attention on the play: each child has a Barbie doll that they dress and make speak to other children's Barbie dolls. Parten suggests that you can observe children in play and actually discover, if you look closely, those who are functioning for the most part at lower levels in the hierarchy.

EXAMPLE IV
The teacher of a fourth-grade girl with Asperger Syndrome remarked to the child's mother that the girl was 'playing' with her friends at recess and did not appear to be having trouble getting along with her peers. On closer observation, however, the mother noted that the child played in close proximity to the other children, frequently dictated directions and/or rules to the others, but did not actually reciprocate play using *their* rules and expectations for play.

Gesell and Ilg (Gesell and Ilg 1946) continue to emphasize this hierarchy. At age seven, children begin to worry about their place in the group, afraid they will not hold their own. At age eight, children begin to accept the fact that their role in the group is to some extent determined by their abilities and limitations. By age nine, the children begin to form informal clubs, short-lived, but more organized in structure. Children who have the ability to enter into groups of play with others with ease tend to become more socially adept with their peers than those who do not have the skills to do so.

o *Children with Asperger Syndrome may have a bland 'affect'*
   (i.e. few facial expressions).

   Teachers and parents report that it may be difficult to tell 'what is going on inside them' because they often do not show their feelings very easily. In fact, as mentioned previously in the DSMIV diagnostic criteria, this difficulty in displaying nonverbal communication is one of the diagnosing characteristics of Asperger Syndrome children.

   EXAMPLE I
   Parents of children with Asperger Syndrome frequently report that at Christmas time and on their child's birthday, they appear to be unimpressed with presents. One after another, presents are opened without any display of joy or surprise. Sometimes there is such a lack of interest that the parents themselves must open the presents for the child. For some children, opening gifts can even be distressing. Not being able to anticipate the contents of a gift may be too disturbing for some children to enjoy the practice.

○ *Children with this diagnosis often can not decipher the facial expressions and body language of other children and adults.*

> EXAMPLE I
>
> A kindergarten student was asked to put the 'weather clock' pointer on the correct weather for the day. Although it was raining, he decided it would be funny if he put the pointer on 'SUNNY.' Much to his delight, the other children laughed; however, his teacher was not amused. She asked him several times to put the pointer on the correct weather, with increasing degrees of sternness. The boy could not 'read' these cues of impatience and continued his little game until he was asked to sit down, away from the group, as punishment for his inappropriate behavior.

○ *Children with Asperger Syndrome may have problems reading nonverbal gestures and cues.*

> EXAMPLE I
>
> A second-grade student has not learned that when a teacher 'zips' his mouth to his class, this means the children should stop talking. He frequently is viewed as noncompliant; when, in actuality, he does not understand the meaning of this nonverbal cue.

Teachers who have children in their classrooms with this diagnosis need to be continually aware of their methods of communication and not take for granted that their students understand nonverbal cues.

o *Children with this diagnosis may have difficulty practicing self-awareness: they may not be aware that their clothes are mismatched, when their hygiene is poor, or when they may be acting obnoxious. They may also not understand why these things are important.*

> EXAMPLE I
>
> One junior-high boy with Asperger Syndrome frequently left the rest-room without pulling up his zipper. Other students began to make remarks and tease him for this habit. The boy had no awareness that this should be an embarrassment to him and even seemed to enjoy the attention he was getting from his peers.

o *Children with Asperger Syndrome may exhibit an inability to control their emotions and their anxieties.*

> EXAMPLE I
>
> Temple Grandin, an adult woman with high-functioning autism writes (Grandin 1995, pp.87–88) 'My childhood temper tantrums were not really expressions of emotion so much as circuit overloads. When I calmed down, the emotion was all over. When I get angry, it is like an afternoon thunderstorm; the anger is intense, but once I get over it, the emotion quickly dissipates.' This author fondly refers to this effect as the 'Richter Scale of Emotions.' Individuals with this disorder can sometimes go from 0–2,000 on the Richter Scale of Emotion.

> EXAMPLE II
>
> Michael, a child with high-functioning autism, seemed to have great difficulty recognizing when he was becoming stressed, until it was too late. Therefore, utilizing 'stress-busters' and calming techniques were ineffective. It was too difficult for him to recognize when he needed to use them. He had to be taught *first* what the signals were that his body would give to him so that he would know when he was becoming stressed.

o *Individuals with this disorder may exhibit poor eye gaze; they may also avoid eye contact in conversation.*

EXAMPLE I

Teddy, a pre-school child with Asperger Syndrome, never faces the speaker in circle time. He appears to be looking out the window or away from the teacher. However, when asked, he can respond appropriately to questions about the material. Indeed, he must have been paying attention after all.

Studies have shown that individuals without disabilities who exhibit poor eye contact frequently have more social problems as well. Interestingly, though, the opposite effect of the speaker displaying too much eye contact in conversation may be uncomfortable for some listeners. Also, if the listener must concentrate too hard on making eye contact with a speaker, it may interfere with his/her ability to understand the message. We should be careful, for this reason, about teaching too much of this skill.

EXAMPLE II

Temple Grandin writes (Grandin 1995, p.73), 'some of the problems autistics have with making eye contact may be nothing more than an intolerance for the movement of the other person's eyes.' Other individuals with this disorder report that they cannot attend to two things at once: listening to an individual's speech and at the same time watching his/her eyes (joint focus of attention). If they do both, they may miss information and not understand what is being said. Some people with autism report that they watch the mouths and not the eyes of the people they are engaging in conversation with.

Individuals with autism may also display other problems with their eyes such as problems with visual tracking and depth perception. This makes it difficult, and possibly dangerous, for them to participate in sports, go up and down stairs or bleachers, or follow someone's point to locate an object. Although it is not the intent of this author to discuss the visual and gross motor difficulties these children may have, it is important to understand that when a child is grossly deficient in sports ability, is a boy, and is in the upper elementary years of age, his self-esteem may suffer. Low self-esteem can certainly impact on proper social behavior. Physical education instructors should always be aware of the potential hazards for children with this diagnosis because of these deficits. If a child can not anticipate a ball being thrown at him and instinctively react to either catch it or protect himself, he will most certainly at one time or another suffer injury. It is unfair to expect such a child to be able to participate fully in physical education classes without some modifications.

○ *Children with high-functioning autism may have trouble 'sharing.' For some, this only serves to enhance the misunderstanding that they are 'selfish' and need discipline. As older children or teenagers, they may find it hard to 'share' their feelings and apprehensions with their peers or their parents.*

EXAMPLE I

A ten-year-old boy looked out his window to see his sister using a ball that he seldom played with, but belonged to him. He ran out of the house screaming, 'That's mine! Give it back!' The sibling, surprised at his intense reaction, immediately handed it over to him. He then promptly dropped it in the grass and went inside.

EXAMPLE II

One teenage boy with Asperger Syndrome ('Bill') reported that during a sleep-over with a friend, the boy proceeded to tell him all about which girls he liked and why. He asked Bill to keep this secret. His secret was safe with Bill, but as Bill told his friend later, he didn't understand why it had to be a secret anyhow. You either like someone or you don't.

○ *Individuals with this disorder may find it hard to seek and offer comfort to others.*

EXAMPLE I
A mother of an eight-year-old boy with Asperger Syndrome was appalled that he did not attempt to help his sister who had caught her arm in the rungs of a chair and was screaming in pain. When the mother ran into the room to assist the girl, the boy remarked casually, 'I wonder how she got her arm caught in there.'

Individuals with Asperger Syndrome sometimes appear to learn to understand human emotions based on intellectualizing them. For example, individuals who are sad will cry; when they are happy, they will smile. Individuals who are angry will yell. However, what happens when one is smiling and at the same time is crying? What happens when a person is angry but is not yelling or even raising his/her voice? Understanding these types of emotions requires much ability to dissect body language and the finer social nuances of communication. This is not to say that all children with this diagnosis have this problem, and some children have it in varying degrees. Some children develop or improve this skill as they get older.

○ *Children with Asperger Syndrome may have difficulty responding to various types of social praise or criticism.*

EXAMPLE I
A teacher of a seventh-grade student with Asperger Syndrome noticed that praise and constructive criticism were often not meaningful to this individual. She noticed that typical students responded to praise, but her student with Asperger Syndrome did not seem to internalize it. She felt that perhaps the student had trouble looking critically at himself to

discover the reason for praise, and thus the reason for constructive criticism as well.

EXAMPLE II

A second-grade child with high-functioning autism was reprimanded by his teacher when she overheard the child calling another student 'bad.' When the teacher scolded him for name-calling, the child with autism felt that he was justified. He could not get past the fact that the other child *was* frequently someone who got into trouble and lost his recess time, etc., for his behavior. The child with autism was oblivious to his own lack of social courtesy. On the flip side, this child also has trouble understanding teasing and distinguishing friendly teasing from harmful teasing when it was applied to him. If he was teased for something, he internalized it and believed it. After all, why would someone say something they don't mean?

EXAMPLE III

One teacher rewarded her students with stickers when they completed their work well. Her student with autism did not enjoy receiving stickers and even seemed to be irritated with having them stuck to his completed worksheets as evidenced by his continual desire to peel them off.

Many of the reward systems that children with autism respond to may remain undiscovered because they are atypical. Parents can be helpful in informing teachers about the types of rewards that work best. Educators may be surprised at the intensity with which children with autism will respond to these atypical motivators! We will discuss this more in Chapter 6.

In conclusion, when a teacher is confronted with the possibility of having a child with Asperger Syndrome or high-functioning autism in his/her classroom, he/she must remember to examine the child's behavior through the lens of the student's disability. Educators need to look for the 'why' of the behavior and examine its possible causes. More often than not, troublesome behaviors, when viewed through the eyes of the disability, will be easier to elimi-nate. Appropriate interventions to encourage acceptable social behavior will become easier to develop. The child will flourish in this kind of accepting environment, and teachers will feel well rewarded in the knowledge that they are truly making a difference in the life of a child with an autism spectrum disorder.

CORRESPONDING LESSON PLANS

Lesson plan 1

IEP goal
Student will be able to demonstrate perspective-taking ability, both indi-vidual and group.

Method of instruction
Small group and individual instruction.

Materials needed
- Blackboard, chalk, and pictures of groups of people who are displaying emotions such as anger, fear, sadness, boredom (it is important that the pictures display a wide variety of emotions). The teacher will also need various pictures of individuals displaying emotions.

Introduction
Boys and girls, we are going to work on recognizing what it feels like to be another person for a minute. Sometimes we refer to this as 'stepping into another person's shoes.' We use this saying when we want to learn what another person is feeling at a particular moment. We want to 'step

into his shoes' and pretend that we are him or her to understand better how he or she feels.

How would you feel if you broke your leg during summer break, had to be in the hospital for three days, and could not go swimming for two months? (Children should describe what they would feel in the hospital and at home.)

Now, let's pretend that one of your classmates has broken his leg and is in the hospital. You would like to go and visit him there. What kinds of things would you say to him when you entered his room? (Encourage the children to think about how the child must feel – he cannot go out and play, his leg probably hurts, he may be having some painful needle sticks, he probably does not care for the food he must eat there, and he may be a bit lonely for his family and friends. The teacher should write appropriate comments on the board.)

Can you tell me some things that might not be appropriate to say to your classmate in the hospital? For example, what if I said, 'I guess I won't be able to ask you to go to the pool with me anymore. I guess I'll have to ask Richey.' (Children should offer more inappropriate comments, the classmates should analyze them as to why they are not appropriate, and the teacher should write these on the board in a separate area. Then they should begin to offer appropriate comments as well.)

There are other ways we should be able to tell how someone is feeling. Sometimes we can tell by looking at their faces and examining their facial expressions. If they are crying, or their cheeks are wet, they may be feeling sad. People who are sad may also blink back tears, look down at the ground, or cover their face with their hands. People who cry may also be in pain. Sometimes, a lot of people might be crying about something as a group. (Encourage the children to talk about how they might know that the group is sad.)

Groups can also display other emotions. Some groups may be angry. (Encourage the children to discuss how they might know if a group is angry.)

Student practice

(Students are divided into pairs. Each pair is given a picture of a group displaying an emotion. They are then asked to examine the picture, identify the emotion, and think about why the group might be displaying this emotion. Each pair should then report on their picture. For instance, striking workers with angry faces might be holding up signs. They may be angry about their jobs.)

Further introduction

(Once the students are able to identify how the people are feeling in the pictures, discussion should continue as to how conversation and behavior should be 'tailored' to match this emotion.)

How many people have ever done poorly on a test or a classwork assignment? How does it make you feel? (Children may share that usually they are sad or embarrassed.)

Some students may be feeling sad about their grade or worried. They are not usually happy or proud. It would not be appropriate to tell a joke about this person's grades, would it? What would you say instead? (Children offer comments again.)

Student practice

1. (The teacher then provides each pair with a picture card of someone displaying an emotion. The pair must identify the emotion, think up two pretend situations that might cause this type of emotion, and then describe two appropriate comments that they could make if the person in the picture was in the room right now. Each pair should then report their responses.)

2. (This time, in pairs as before, the children are given a different group situation card. They are to look at the card and come up with an appropriate comment if they were to enter the room where this group was. Each pair should report their responses. [Note: One teacher used a picture from the movie *Titanic*.])

Additional practice for the student with Asperger Syndrome

1. (A walk down the hall with the student could be arranged. The child could be instructed to peek into the windows of certain classrooms and identify the feeling that the children in the room are exhibiting at that one particular moment: boredom, interest, happiness. They should also try to identify or offer a 'guess' based on their observations, as to what might be causing it.)

2. (The teacher should be on the lookout for inappropriate comments or reactions to different perspectives. For instance, one teacher observed that a when a child was hurt in gym, the student with autism noticed the crying child but did not seem to know what to do about it. This student should be prompted later to see if he/she understood that the child was hurt, i.e. Was the child crying? Was he rubbing his knee? Then the student should be provided a response to memorize and use the next time someone gets hurt. For instance, the student can be coached to approach the hurt child and say, 'Can I help you?')

Parental practice

1. Parents should continue the exercise of perspective-taking:

   a. Have the child watch audience reactions on a talk show without the sound to tell if he/she is able to grasp the perspective of the group. Some of the programs on *Court TV* provide excellent examples of perspective-taking ability. The child can be asked to watch the facial expressions of the judge (without the sound) and guess which party is going to win his/her case.

   b. Have the child draw a picture of how an animal might look when it is hungry and lost.

   c. Have the child look through the comics and cut out pictures of characters that might look frustrated.

Lesson plan 2

Children with Asperger Syndrome and high-functioning autism may have unusual preoccupations as discussed in Chapter 6. These preoccupations can be used as motivators to help the student improve his/her social skills. Below, is an example of a lesson plan devised for a child with a preoccupation with the presidents of the United States. This lesson plan will enable the child to participate in appropriate play with his/her peers. It will also serve to boost his/her self-esteem and encourage respect from his/her peers.

IEP goal
Student will be able to engage in appropriate play with his/her peers.

Method of instruction
Small group.

Materials needed
- Four bases labeled 1, 2, 3, and 'home', arranged as in baseball. At least 30 trivia questions about the presidents of the United States.

Introduction
Today we are going to play a game of trivia. (Explain rules.)

Student practice
(This is a game for up to ten students. It is suggested that the child with Asperger Syndrome be appointed as 'Player 5' of one of the two teams to allow for his/her maximum participation. The rules of the game are as follows:

1.   Divide the class into two teams of five players. Assign each player on each team a number 1–5, and arrange the children on each team in numerical order.

2. Explain to the teams that each team will be asked a question regarding the presidents of the United States.

3. If the team can answer the question correctly, then Player 1 moves to first base. Then, the next team must answer a different question correctly and can send their Player 1 to first base as well [players share bases]. If the teams miss the question, no players are sent to first base from their team.

4. If the team correctly answers the second question, their Player 1 moves to second base, and their Player 2 moves to first base. [Players on bases may not help answer questions.] Proceed with new question to the other team and follow this procedure for their Player 1 and 2 as well. If either team misses the question, and they have no players on bases, then their Player 2 does not go to first base. [You must answer a question correctly to send a player to a new base. For all future questions, if the team answers the question correctly, all players from that team move to the next base.]

5. The first team is given their third question. If the remaining players not on bases can answer the question correctly, then Player 3 moves to the team's first available base. The same procedure is followed for Team 2. If the answer is wrong, no players move from that team.

6. Team 1 is given their fourth question. If the remaining players not on bases can answer the question correctly, they send a person to first base and move the team members they have on bases to the next base. When a team member moves to 'home' base, the team scores one point. The same procedure is followed for Team 2.

7. Continue this procedure for remaining team members of each team.

8. Game ends when there are no more questions. The team with the most points wins.)

Additional practice for the student with Asperger Syndrome

(Later, the student with Asperger Sydrome can be assigned to work with another student, or perhaps two other students, to complete a project involving the presidents of the US. This should happen after the game above so that typical peers will see the value in working with this child to complete the project.)

Lesson plan 3

IEP goal

The student will be able to use facial expressions and nonverbal communication correctly in individual and small group instruction.

Materials needed

- A mirror hung on a board with various pictures of children displaying various facial expressions, arranged in circular fashion around it, a deck of cards with an emotion word such as 'happy', 'sad', or 'angry' printed on each card, popular children's stories, age-appropriate.

Introduction

Boys and girls, it is important that we be able to recognize and use facial expressions and body language so that we can understand how people are feeling. Body language is the way we use our bodies to talk without saying words. For example, if someone is reading a story and I respond by yawning (demonstrate), what does this tell the person who is reading a story? (Solicit responses.) What does it tell a person when I frown and fold my arms across my chest like this? (Solicit responses.) Let's see if you can practice some nonverbal communication. I want you to choose a card from this deck and 'act out' the identifying feeling. (If the children can't read, the words can be whispered in their ears.)

Student practice

(Each child should then pick a card with an emotion written on it and begin to act out the emotion with facial expressions and body language [no words permitted]. For example, provide the sample that if the child has picked an 'angry' card, he can pound the desk.)

Further introduction

There are other types of body language that we use to communicate. For example, the sign where we zip our mouth means to be quiet (demonstrate) and so does the sign where we put our index finger to our lips (demonstrate). Pointing to a chair can mean 'sit down.' The sign where we extend our palm straight out means 'stop' (demonstrate), so does the sign where we make a 't' for 'time out' with our hands in front of our chest (demonstrate). Can you think of some others? (Children share others.) What would this body language mean if someone did it to you? (Shake your head from side to side and frown at one of the students to communicate that you want the student to stop doing something.)

It is possible for us to express by the tone and loudness of our voice our feelings as well. For instance, when we are angry, we tend to yell or talk loudly. When we are sad, we may talk quietly and slowly.

Student practice

1. (Each child should then pick an emotion card again. This time, they can use their voices to express the emotions and their bodies. Critique their use of nonverbal communication and offer improvements where necessary.)

2. (Next, on a lighter note, using a popular children's short story, children take turns reading the story using one *inappropriate* emotion (sad, happy, angry). This helps to show how much the meaning of a story can change when the wrong emotion is used.)

Additional practice for the student with Asperger Sydrome
(Using the board with mirrors and pictures as described above, instruct the student to look in the mirror and imitate the various expressions. The instructor should encourage him/her to use his/her fingers to trace the outline of his/her eyebrows and mouth as he/she makes the expressions to enable a simultaneous visual and tactile teaching experience. The instructor can then play a guessing game with the child where the child must guess the teacher's expression.)

Parental practice

1. Parents can and should continue the mirror practice at home.

2. Parents can also cut pictures of eyes out of magazines that are displaying various emotions. The child with Asperger Syndrome should then practice 'reading' the emotions in the eyes and describing them.

3. Using a book, the child should practice reading out loud using appropriate facial expressions. If the child is unable to read, the parent can interrupt the story by asking the child, 'This sounds like a sad part, how should we make our faces look?' Then, the parent can continue reading the story, reinforcing the appropriate facial expressions and body language.

Lesson plan 4

IEP goal
Student will demonstrate improvement in the ability to read facial expressions.

Method of instruction
Small group and individual practice.

Materials needed

- Blackboard and chalk, handout entitled: 'How do you feel today?' (Figure 3.1) and emotion situation cards (Figures 3.2–3.5), one for each student. Also, VCR and VCR tape of various television characters who are demonstrating a variety of facial expressions such as happiness, sadness, fear, anger. The tape should also include more complex ones such as what 'stress' may look like, or 'jealousy.'

Introduction

In order to get along with your classmates, teachers, and parents, it is necessary to be able to understand when they are happy, sad, angry, stressed, etc., and then adjust your responses to match their emotions. For instance, when a person is happy, the corners of his/her mouth usually go up and form a smile. (Draw a smile on the board.) What happens when someone is sad? (Elicit volunteers to demonstrate what a sad face looks like, and then draw it on the board.) Now class, how would you look when you open your favorite birthday present that you have waited many months to get? Let's see you demonstrate it! (Classmates should form their faces to show 'delight'. Teacher should then attempt to display this on the board.) There are other ways we can learn which emotions people are feeling. For instance, happy people may dance around! They use their body to show their happiness. Or they may use their voice. (Demonstrate.) What do you think people who are mad do? (Students should volunteer that they may clench their fist or their teeth, or stamp their feet.) Let's see if you can recognize some other emotions. Some of these may be tricky! (Teacher passes out handout, Figure 3.1: How do you feel today? see p.71)

Student practice

1. (Students examine the handout and identify various situations when they may have seen someone display a particular facial expression. For example, 'hot' may be used when you have run up and down the street on a warm and sunny day or when you are thirsty and want to jump in a cool swimming pool. Students

should mimic the expression as they describe ways to identify with it.)

2.   (Students watch the videotape without audio and try to guess which emotion the character is displaying. Teacher should pause between each character and refer them to their handout above to discover the emotion. After all characters' emotions have been identified, rewind the tape and play it with audio to see if they were correct.)

3.   (Students are then given a card with an emotion written on it, as well as a short situation to act out for their classmates. For instance:

Students should then take turns acting out the situation without words, encouraging the class to guess the emotion *only when he/she is completely through*.)

Additional practice for the student with Asperger Syndrome

(Later, the teacher can identify with the student other situations when a classmate is displaying an emotion. Or, he/she can provide a prompt when someone is displaying one of these emotions. The teacher might say, 'Class, I am getting frustrated with your behavior. How can you tell?' The students can then discuss how this emotion is perceived by body language. He/she can also have the child silently observe children from a distance as they play and try to identify those feelings in certain children, for example playing 'I Spy' or 'Sherlock Holmes' with the child.

Other teachers should try to incorporate the goal as well throughout the week.)

Parental practice

Parents can be provided an assignment to complete during the week to work on this goal with their child. Three emotions cards, similar to the above, can be given to the child to take home. For instance:

Parents should then encourage the child to think of a situation that would produce the emotion and write it on the card. They should

Figure 3.1 How do you feel today?

practice displaying the emotion one at a time, adult first, so that the child can model him/her. Parents should report back to the teacher any problem areas so that the teacher can continue to focus on the goal.

FEAR

You are almost asleep in your room, when suddenly, you hear a strange noise.

Figure 3.2

GUILTY

Figure 3.3

EXHAUSTED

Figure 3.4

RELIEVED

Figure 3.5

Lesson plan 5

IEP goal
Student will be able to demonstrate self-awareness by labeling his/her feelings correctly.

Method of instruction
Small group and/or individual instruction.

Materials needed

- Copies of the story below, one for each student, blackboard and chalk, 'Feelings' handouts.

Introduction
Everyone experiences different types of feelings. Feelings can be positive (which means they are good feelings), or negative (which means they are bad feelings). Feelings have causes. Sometimes our feelings are brought on because we did not interpret the situation correctly. Everyone must learn to identify the feelings they have so that they can let adults and others help them. This will help them to be able to get along with others.

Pass out the following story for the students to read:

'Today at breakfast, my mom ran out of my favorite cereal, and I had to eat a cereal I hate. Then, when I got on the bus, my favorite seat was taken. I heard the class bully say, 'Oh no! Here comes the idiot! You better not sit in this seat!' I had to because there were no other empty seats. When I got to school, I realized that I forgot my bag lunch. Later, I got an 'A' on my science test and the teacher said, 'Good job!' She put my paper on the bulletin board. At lunch time, I had to eat the school lunch because I forgot my bag lunch. It was terrible! At recess, a kid in my class called me a name. In gym class, my shoe fell off when I kicked the ball, and everyone laughed. Later, at home, I relaxed on my pillow and read a book.'

(While the students are reading the story, the teacher should write the following feelings on the blackboard):

fear	**embarrassment**
frustration	**anxiety**
happiness	**contentment**
pride	**anger**
sadness	**excitement**

(When the students are done reading the story, read each line of the story and have the class identify the word above that might describe what the character is feeling. Some lines may actually have two interpretations. Discuss with the student which feelings make us feel 'bad' and which feelings make us feel 'good'. Identify lines that may have feelings that we could change.)

(At this point, pass out to the students the handout about feelings. The handout should contain ten 'situations' where the student can decide an appropriate feeling and write this feeling in a second column beside the first column. Try to use some of the situations you used in your class presentation so that the child with Asperger Syndrome has a point of reference. For instance):

Table 3.1

Situation	Feeling Word
your favorite video game is broken	sadness
your mom asks you to clean your room in the middle of your favorite TV show	frustration
you receive a toy you've always wanted on your birthday	

(Discuss the situations with the class when the handouts seem to be completed. Make note of how some children may have different responses to the situations when choosing a feeling.)

When we use words to describe our feelings, we help others to know when they may be upsetting us, when we are sad or angry, and how they can help us. It may also help them to be able to respond appropriately to us.

(Tell the students you are going to role-play for them a situation where you were playing with your favorite video game, and then it broke. Ask if they can identify your feelings. Role-play for them anger.)

(Next, tell the students you are going to do the same situation and role-play another emotion: disappointment. Ask if someone would like to volunteer to role-play the same situation with the feeling of 'sadness,' but choose the child with Asperger Syndrome.)

(Next, have the students use their words to describe their feelings in the above situations with volunteer role-players.)

If you broke your game before school, came to class feeling angry because of it, do you think your friends would be able to tell *why* you were in a bad mood? No! It's important to express your feelings so people can understand why you feel the way you feel.

Additional practice for the student with Asperger Sydrome
(During the course of the week, encourage the student to identify his/her emotions, especially when he/she appears troubled. This might be done by pointing to a picture of how he/she feels, or drawing a circle on a digit from 1–10 to identify the *degree* of the emotion if he/she cannot express it.)

Parental practice
At home, students should keep a 'feelings' diary for for four days. Parents should have the child describe the various situations during the day when these feelings might have been experienced:

sadness   **anger**

frustration   **happiness**

loneliness   **fear**

Parents should also encourage the child to label his/her feelings with words, especially during times when he/she is upset. At first, the parent may need to supply the label for the child: 'I see that you are angry about something. Tell me what it is.'

Lesson plan 6

IEP goal

The student will be able to demonstrate good listening skills – including eye contact.

Materials needed

- 'Jim's Banana Split' handout (see Figure 3.6) and crayons for each student, tape, two laminated cards with the five 'Good Listening' skills listed below, a weekly calendar chart, stickers, blackboard, chalk.

Introduction

Boys and girls, today we are going to talk about good listening skills. Good listening is important because it helps us to be able to follow directions. Good listening is more than being able to answer questions after we have listened to someone talk.

Good listening also involves demonstrating good body language.

Does anyone know what body language is? (Solicit responses.) Body language is the way we use our bodies to talk *without* using words. For instance, when you are listening to a really boring speaker, how might your body look? (Students should volunteer slouched positions, head resting on one hand, looking off into space, etc.) Now, how might you show me with your body that a speaker really interests you? (Students should sit up straight, look interested, display good eye contact.) Great! Did you know that demonstrating good listening skills also makes speakers feel important? Speakers always enjoy talking when people make them feel as if what they say is really interesting. Children also like to talk to other children who listen and pay attention to them when they speak. Being a good friend means being a good listener. Here are five things you should remember to do when you want to be a good listener (write these on the board):

1. Look at the speaker.

2. Sit up tall in your chair.

3. Face the speaker.

4. Nod when you agree with the speaker, or smile when the speaker smiles.

5. Raise your hand politely when you want to ask a question.

Student practice

Boys and girls, we are going to practice a listening exercise. A friend of mine, Jim, needs your help. He recently got a job at an ice cream shop. His boss has to leave the shop because of an emergency and is leaving Jim in charge. He never taught Jim how to make a banana split, so he is going to teach him now. You will need to help Jim remember everything, okay? Can you demonstrate good listening skills? (Review 1–5 again above.)

This is what Jim's boss said:

'Jim, I will be gone an hour and a half. I never had the time to teach you how to make a banana split, so I am going to review that with you now quickly. You can do it, I'm sure. First, you will need to find the banana split dishes, they are the long yellow ones. Put three piles of ice cream in the dish: one on each end, and one in the middle. Take a banana, peel it, and cut it in half. Wrap one half in plastic wrap so that it doesn't get brown. Take the other half and cut it in half lengthwise. (Mime for the students as you speak, so that students will have the visual reminder as well.) Put each half on either side of the ice cream piles. Next, put chocolate syrup on one pile, pineapple syrup on the middle pile, and strawberry syrup on the last pile. Take one scoop of nuts and spread them on the whole dessert. Spray some whipped cream on each individual icecream pile. Now, top each pile off with a cherry. Thanks Jim, I'll be back!'

As soon as Jim's boss left, a customer came into the shop and ordered a banana split. Can you help Jim?

(At this point, students should use their recall of the story to draw a banana split using Figure 3.6 handouts. When they are through, they should tape them onto the blackboard.)

Additional student practice

(The teacher should point out and review from the taped pictures the students' work and how they followed the directions of the story.)

Let's see if you were good listeners!

1. What color were the banana split dishes that Jim should use?

2. How many piles of ice cream should go in the dish?

3. How should Jim cut the bananas?

4. What types of syrup should Jim put on top of the ice cream piles?

5. What goes on the ice cream after the syrup?

6. What is sprayed on the ice cream?

7. What fruit should he use in the end? Where does it go?

8. When will Jim's boss be back?

Additional practice for the student with Asperger Syndrome

(The student with Asperger Syndrome should be provided with a laminated card of the five 'Good Listening' skills above to keep on his/her desk. When he/she is doing a good job, the teacher can reward him/her by putting a sticker on his/her weekly calendar chart. Ideally, the calendar chart should have large squares to accommodate several stickers a day. If the student is not displaying good listening skills, the

Figure 3.6 Jim's Banana Split

teacher can discreetly point to his/her chart when walking by his/her desk.)

Parental practice

Parents should review the sticker chart weekly with the student and praise him/her for progress. The parent should also be provided a laminated card with the 'Good Listening' skills so that they can prompt the child as well.

Lesson plan 7

IEP goal

The student will be able to adjust the volume of his/her voice when provided with a visual prompt.

Materials needed

- 'Voice volume gauge' (Figure 3.7), blackboard, and chalk.

Introduction

Sometimes we must use a quiet voice in school, for instance, when we are completing worksheets or tests in class, or listening to the teacher give directions. When we are walking in the halls, we must also use a quiet voice so that we do not disturb other classes. Other times, it is okay for us to use a loud voice. For instance, when we are outside on the playground at recess, or when we are in physical education class. When your voice is too loud, and it is not appropriate, I will draw a picture for you of where you are on a 'voice gauge' and then another one of where you need to be. For instance, right now, my voice is at a '3' (draw the voice gauge on the blackboard with the needle at '3'). If I talk louder, the gauge may change to a '5'. (Draw this for the student). Let's practice using your voice.

Student practice

(The teacher should draw the 'voice gauge' with the gauge at various volumes and ask the student to speak a short phrase at each level of volume. She should have the student give examples of when these volumes are appropriate in the school day and have the child rehearse volumes at various levels. It may be easier for the student to begin practice by saying the phrase at the lowest level of volume and then building up to the highest level.)

Additional student practice

(Eventually, when the student responds well to the visual prompt, the prompt can be faded and replaced with an auditory prompt, such as having the student adjust the volume of his/her voice when he/she hears the desired 'number' being called out by the teacher.)

Parental practice

Parents can continue this method at home, teaching the student appropriate voice volumes for activities as they apply at home. For instance, playing outside versus watching television indoors.

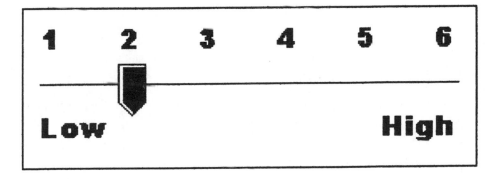

Figure 3.7 Voice volume gauge

CHAPTER FOUR

Sensory Differences in Children with Autism and Asperger Syndrome

'My reflection is clear in the center, wrinkled near the edges,
ragged on the outside.
I can force myself to see only the clear,
I can focus my eyes on the middle,
The essence,
The point from which clarity comes...'

— Liane Holliday Willey

Children with autism and Asperger Syndrome may experience a variety of sensory integration problems. Dr. Nancy Minshew, a prominant researcher in the brain function of high-functioning autistics at the University of Pittsburgh Medical Center, states: 'Sensory sensitivities relate to impairment in higher cortical sensory perception (how the brain interprets basic sensory phenomena) – the problems [with sensory integration] arise because of difficulty with information processing.' These sensory differences can sometimes prevent appropriate social interactions.

As many teachers have discovered, to be successful, treatment plans for children with a diagnosis of Asperger Syndrome must take into account their sensory problems. 'All the behavior modification in the world is not going to stop a child from screaming if the sound of the bell hurts' (Quill 1995, p.39).

The following are examples of areas where sensory processing may be of concern:

- sound sensitivity

- touch sensitivity

- visual perception

- taste distortions

- problems with the sense of smell

- rhythm difficulties

- vestibular differences

- problems with proprioception.

Family members can certainly supply information about these difficulties to educators and should be looked upon as a resource for this type of information. Schools should make the teachers aware of the student's problems, as well as any other staff members that may interact with him/her. Teaching instruction may need to be modified so that certain sensory inputs are eliminated. Sensory integration therapy (a branch of occupational therapy) may help children with these differences to become desensitized to problem areas and allow them to learn to regulate their behaviors.

I. SOUND SENSITIVITY

Children with autism and Asperger Syndrome may exhibit a sensitivity to certain volumes or pitches in sound. They may be so sensitive that certain sounds are painful to their ears and may display their anguish by attempting to cover their ears, hiding, and/or taking on a 'pained' expression. We can all relate to the very disturbing sound of fingernails scratching across a blackboard, and many of us shudder just at the *anticipation* of such a noise. For children with this disorder, other sounds may cause them problems as well. High-pitched singing voices, crying babies, flushing toilets, fire alarm bells, vacuum cleaners, blow dryers, washing machines, and blenders produce sounds that frequently are reported as troublesome for children with this disorder. If the child is experiencing pain involving certain sounds, he/she will not be able to address his/her social deficits.

EXAMPLE I
A mother reports that her son is terrified at the sound of the fire alarm and has made all the staff at school aware of this problem. When there is a drill, the boy is removed from the building before the warning bell sounds. One day, a substitute was present in the boy's class. The bell began to ring. At once, the boy threw himself on the floor, covered his ears, and screamed in pain. It was impossible to get him to leave the building with the other children. For the next week, when the school bus pulled up in front of the school, the child bolted for the nearby woods because he was afraid to enter the building. The desensitizing process took several additional days to allow him even to be able to enter the school.

EXAMPLE II
Another family reports that their son is extremely sensitive to the lead singer's voice of the rock group, *Meatloaf.* They noticed that whenever *Meatloaf* was playing on the radio, their son would begin to scream and cover his ears. One day, the child was having his teeth cleaned in a dentist's office. He was cooperating peacefully when *Meatloaf* began to

play on the speaker. He jumped up from the chair and ran into the waiting room holding his ears and crying. On another occasion, he was asleep on the couch while his parents watched a late night talk show. *Meatloaf* was the guest band on the show. When they began to play, the boy immediately woke and began to scream in pain.

EXAMPLE III

An unnerved physical education teacher called a parent of a child with Asperger Syndrome to explain how her child was fully cooperating in a game the teacher had devised involving the imitation of animal sounds. When she called out 'bird', the children began to imitate bird noises. The child with Asperger Syndrome began to hold his ears and cry. He could not be consoled until he was removed from the gym. The boy's mother then explained to the teacher that he could not tolerate bird noises.

Some individuals with autism report that their hearing may fade in and out, becoming louder or softer at times as if someone was adjusting the volume knob on a radio. For others, background noises may sound just as loud as noises close by.

Physical education teachers should also be aware that the echoes produced in a gymnasium or in small rooms such as locker rooms or bathrooms are also frequent problem areas for these children. Loud, confusing areas, such as cafeterias, recess rooms, etc., may also produce troubling behaviors because some of these children have difficulty filtering out background noises. They may not be able to follow instructions or directions under such conditions. For instance, the 'hum' of fluorescent lighting fixtures may distract a student so much that he can not tune into directions. Some children may hum or make noises of their own to block out disturbing sounds. For example, several children the author has become familiar with hum during their meals because the noise of crunchy foods bothers them.

II. TOUCH SENSITIVITIES

Frequently, children with this diagnosis may be unable to tolerate the feel of the tags on their clothing. Bras, denim cloth, zippers, rivets, buttons, etc., may also produce a problem. Their skin may actually develop welts when exposed to the above because they are so hypersensitive. Children may avoid wearing certain types of clothing. These avoidance behaviors are not to be compared with those of typical children with clothing preferences. Their behaviors may be severe and extreme. They would rather endure punishment than wear the offensive clothing. Some parents of teenagers report that it is difficult for their sons and daughters with this diagnosis to wear deodorants or lotions. This can certainly interfere with their social success.

EXAMPLE I

A kindergarten student was instructed by his teacher to zip his coat before going out for recess. The boy refused. When the teacher insisted and zipped the coat herself, the boy reacted violently by kicking her. The parent later explained that the child cannot tolerate the feel of the zipper against his neck. He must wear his coat unzipped at all times.

EXAMPLE II

One boy with Asperger Syndrome refuses to wear jeans because he can not tolerate the feel of the rivets inside against his skin. His mother must cover them with soft felt before he will wear them.

EXAMPLE III

One mother did not realize the extent of the pain her child suffered when the tags were left inside his clothes. After much complaining by the child, she checked his neck to discover welts created by a tag that had already been laundered several times and probably would not have bothered someone else.

Children with Asperger Syndrome may also react violently when touched by other children and adults. In particular, they may be more sensitive to light touches than deep-pressure touches. Frequently, these children prefer to sit on the end of tables or be the last in line so that they can avoid this unpleasant sensation. Indeed, placing a child at the end of the line may be beneficial if a student with this diagnosis is having trouble standing in line without problems.

EXAMPLE IV
Liane Holliday Willey writes (Willey 1999, p.21) that she was asked to leave her ballet class when she was six years old because she kept hitting the other children. When her mother asked her why she did this, she replied, 'Because they touched me.'

It has also been reported by parents that children with this disorder may have difficulty comprehending what their body temperature is (whether they are too hot or cold) and what to do to remedy it. For instance, they may not wear proper seasonal clothing because they don't feel the heat or the cold. When they are cold, they may not put on a coat. On the flip side, when they are hot, they may not take off clothes that may be causing them to become overheated.

III. VISUAL PERCEPTION WEAKNESSES

Some children with autism have difficulty with depth perception. For this reason, teachers may need to be aware of the dangers in this child going up and down bleachers or navigating stairs. Others share that they avoid looking at moving objects or that they prefer to use peripheral vision rather than looking at something head on. For these individuals, peripheral vision is more reliable. Certain colors or patterns may also be painful or cause visual problems for some. It is not that the eyes function improperly, it is that the visual information that is received by the eyes is not processed correctly.

EXAMPLE I
One adult woman reports that she can not pull a car into a garage if there is already another car in it as she cannot judge how to avoid hitting it.

It should also be noted that fluorescent lighting may be painful for some children with Asperger Syndrome. Liane Holliday Willey writes (Willey 1999 p.113) that she frequently had to wear sunglasses indoors because the overhead lights hurt her eyes.

IV. TASTE DISTORTIONS

Some individuals may complain that certain textures or tastes are bothersome. This is different from the child who demonstrates avoidance of certain foods. These children may eliminate entire food groups, become nauseated if forced to eat them, exhibit strong avoidance behaviors, and adopt 'food jags' where the child will eat only one type of food for weeks. Frequently, they may have to participate in feeding problem programs to help them become desensitized to the foods that bother them. Toothpaste, mouthwash, vitamins, and certain oral medications may also be disdained. As a side note, however, some children with autism enjoy eating foods that other children may find intolerable.

EXAMPLE I
One ten-year old boy with Asperger Syndrome enjoys sucking on lemon slices. He does not 'pucker' as typical children and adults would do when experiencing the bitterness.

V. PROBLEMS WITH THE SENSE OF SMELL

Educators who work with children with Asperger Syndrome frequently say that certain smells may trigger reactions. The children may become nauseated or have increased motor activity because they are reacting to the odors of hairspray, deodorant, perfumes, room fresheners, insect sprays, etc. Teachers should be aware that classrooms located near bathrooms, janitor closets, or cafeterias may invoke reactions. Teachers should avoid wearing perfume or scented hair spray until such problems have been ruled out.

EXAMPLE I
One girl with Asperger Syndrome is unable to attend church because the mingling odors of cigarette smoke on clothing, perfume, hairspray, and incense make her sick.

EXAMPLE II
One 12-year-old boy with autism must have alternative transportation to school because the school bus exhaust fumes cause him to vomit with each ride to and from the building.

VI. RHYTHM DIFFICULTIES

Individuals with Asperger Syndrome may have problems following a rhythm. They may exhibit 'perfect pitch' but cannot clap to a beat or use rhythm instruments in synchronization (O'Connell 1974). Temple Grandin, an adult woman with autism, reports that it is difficult for her to follow the rhythm of conversation. She explains that she has trouble knowing when to enter a conversation, and frequently she breaks in at inappropriate times and interrupts. She has difficulty knowing how long a pause should last and when it is appropriate to end a pause by speaking.

EXAMPLE I

One music teacher shares a story of how a third-grade student with Asperger Syndrome was always 'off-beat' when participating in a clapping music activity. The other children would become frustrated because he would then throw the others off as well.

VII. VESTIBULAR DIFFERENCES

One can think of vestibular differences as interfering with one's sense of balance, which is controlled through the functions of the inner ear. But the vestibular system also allows us to coordinate our eye movements with our head movements. We know of many people who suffer from motion-sickness. Some individuals report that they do not enjoy amusement park rides because they become dizzy or nauseated. They may avoid riding in elevators because they do not like the feel of rising and falling as the elevator moves up or down. Some may need to hold banisters tightly when they descend stairs. For others, walking on a balance beam or even heel-to-heel on a straight line is impossible. The vestibular system also affects our ability to hold our head while we track a ball coming towards us, follow a point, or copy work from a blackboard.

EXAMPLE I

A young boy with autism was terrified to navigate a tall flight of steps in his school, especially when the stairwell was filled with many children trying to go up and down the staircase at once. His classroom assistant had to escort the child to recess several minutes before the other children so that he could descend the stairs by himself, holding her hand and the banister tightly.

EXAMPLE II

A fifth-grade boy seemed to have much difficulty holding his head up – he would frequently slouch in his chair, or put his head down on the desk.

His teacher wondered if he was getting enough sleep. His muscle tone was low, and he seemed to tire easily. Upon examination, an occupational therapist discovered he had severe problems with his vestibular functioning.

VIII. PROBLEMS WITH PROPRIOCEPTION

Proprioception is defined as the sense that allows us to locate our body position in space. Phyllis Malone, a physical therapist in Pittsburgh, Pennsylvania, who works in an early intervention program, describes a test she uses for discovering children who may have proprioception problems. She instructs the child to close his/her eyes and extend his/her arms straight out. She then asks the child to lift one of the arms up slightly. Then, she instructs the child to lift the other arm up to match it, with eyes still closed. Children with proprioception problems may have difficulty with this exercise. To compensate, they may have to be taught how to reach developmental milestones in a step-by-step fashion the way other children learn to do these things more naturally. For instance learning to throw a ball or using utensils correctly and exerting the right amount of pressure to have them work may be hard for children with autism. Coordinating our body movements is extremely difficult if the parts of our muscles that send messages to our brains are not working efficiently. These children may actually have to learn the individual movements required to complete very simple physical tasks like combing their hair, brushing their teeth, or snapping their coats. They may also be messy eaters, unable to sit still for long, fixate on spinning objects, or crave rocking or rotary motion.

EXAMPLE I
One student will avoid climbing playground equipment at recess because he is unsure of his body's positions above ground and has a fear that he will fall.

EXAMPLE II
Liane Holliday Willey (Willey 1999, p.34) writes that she could not follow her aerobic teacher's instructions unless she placed herself directly behind her, imitating her motions.

EXAMPLE III
One child with autism greets other children by running into them at full force, knocking them down, and hugging them tightly. He appears to be unaware that his touch is too strong.

EXAMPLE IV
Before her son was diagnosed with autism, one parent reported to her son's pediatrician that he could never 'find' an airplane or a bird in the sky when she pointed it out to him.

For some children, problems with the vestibular and proprioceptive systems may exist together. For instance consider the child who can not get off and on an escalator – holding one foot up in the air and balancing himself while he anticipates the next rise of the escalator stair is too just difficult.

In conclusion, the sensory integration problems of these children may range from mild to severe. They may exist in one area or several. These children may need to have adaptations to their school and home environments, or they may be able to go without them. It is important that these problems be treated with care and understanding by parents and teachers, as well as by their peers. The adaptations that are made to allow for these differences may be critical to the social success as well as the academic success of children with Asperger Syndrome in inclusive education settings.

STRATEGIES FOR TEACHING

The most important strategy for dealing with the sensory problems of children with Asperger Syndrome is to *become aware of them*. If the child is experiencing sensory difficulties, he/she may soon begin to overload, making learning of any type difficult. There may be an increase in self-stimulatory behaviors such as spinning, flapping, and pacing, as the child attempts to calm himself. When you see this occurring, try to remove the child from his/her present environment to a place where it is calmer and quieter. An increase in negative behaviors should also be considered as a possible result of sensory overload. Remember that some of these children may be having behavior problems simply because they are *anticipating* a painful stimulation of their senses.

Allow for the child to have a safe place to retreat to when he/she needs to. Such a place can be referred to as a 'quiet spot' or a 'safe spot.' 'Safe spots' can be created within the classroom by a partition, or even a sheet draped over a small table. Some big pillows placed in this area with some head phones will enable the child to 'tune the world out' for a few minutes to regroup. Sleeping bags also serve this purpose. You will know the child is ready to rejoin the group when he/she can complete a small task successfully – a puzzle, or a paper and pencil maze activity. Other students, as well, could benefit from a 'quiet spot' from time to time. A 'quiet spot' should differ from a 'time-out' spot so that the 'quiet spot' is not referred to as being used by children who are bad (Fouse and Wheeler 2000). If the child has become completely out of hand, vigorous exercise may be helpful. A brisk walk, run, or swing is sometimes useful. Jumping on a trampoline or bouncing on a large ball can serve to release anxiety and also help with proprioceptive problems. Deep pressure exercises can also be calming for some children. For instance, wrapping the child in a gym mat has proven successful for some, or relaxing in a large beanbag chair. There also exist on the market weighted vests that children can put on when they are becoming stressed. The same effect can be achieved by wearing a heavy backpack. However, it should be noted that for some, deep pressure exercises are not enjoyable and may cause further behavior problems.

You can create some calming devices to use when a child needs help learning to relax:

- Take an empty clear plastic water bottle, fill it with a cup of clear Karo syrup using a funnel, and add some glitter. Put some glue on the ridges of the lid and screw it back on the bottle. When the student is becoming stressed, have him/her tilt the bottle back and forth and focus his/her eyes on the glitter as it moves through the syrup. This may help him/her to relax.

- Obtain a good quality balloon. Wrap the mouth of the balloon around the bottom of a funnel and add rice, tapping the balloon gently on the table to eliminate air pockets. When the balloon is full, tie it off in a knot. The student can then squeeze the balloon when he/she becomes stressed. You can also make the same device using flour instead of rice. Both items will also help with building hand strength.

Encouraging the child to push or pull heavy objects occasionally, or perform tasks where they must carry a heavy object for a short amount of time, can help with proprioceptive problems.

Children with sensory problems may exhibit excessive and repetitive behaviors (rocking, spinning, hand flicking, head banging). These may be classic symptoms that their sensory systems are in overload. However, some children crave these sensations because their sensory systems are *understimulated*. You will need to look closely to determine if the repetitive behavior is a result of stress, or if they are craving vestibular stimulation. Allowing the child to have *controlled* periods of spinning or rocking will be beneficial as a 'stress buster,' and may also serve to increase needed stimulation to the vestibular system.

For children with visual/spacial problems, use calming lights and remove objects that dangle from the ceilings or flap in the wind from your room's decor. Use muted, soft colors. Replace flickering light bulbs. Avoid seating the child in a high-traffic area such as near a pencil sharpener or garbage can. If the child is having trouble attending to a worksheet, eliminate articles on his/her desk. Provide a black or dark-colored background under the worksheet. Place the worksheet on a vertical surface which will draw it closer to his/her eyes.

For children with auditory problems, try closing the door to the classroom during a quiet period of the day and 'tune-in' to the noises that you hear within your room. Choose seating away from the noises you cannot eliminate. Warn the child if sudden noises are expected. Applying felt to the bottoms of chair feet may help to eliminate 'scratching' sounds. Limiting the use of a pencil sharpener or other noisy appliance in the classroom will be helpful.

For students with tactile defensiveness problems, it may be necessary to avoid having him/her finger paint, use clay, or apply glue with his/her hands. Have him/her use tools such as cookie cutters or Q-tips to complete the task. If the child has difficulty sitting in a group setting, allow a small rug or taped-off portion of the sitting area to be 'his' or 'her' space.

Occupational therapy should have a sensory component to address the needs of these children. Sensory integration therapy may help the child with vestibular differences, touch sensitivities, and visual/perception problems. It may also serve to reduce the amount of stress the child feels because of his/her sensory differences.

CHAPTER FIVE

Social Skills Assessment Tools

Samples and Descriptions

> 'The fisher who draws in his net too soon,
> Won't have any fish to sell;
> The child who shuts up his book too soon,
> Won't learn any lessons well...'
>
> — Unknown

Now that we understand the basic social behavior, social communication, and sensory processing differences of children with Asperger Syndrome and high-functioning autism, our next task will be to design an appropriate intervention program. The first step in any intervention program is to identify by assessment weak areas that will serve as ground points for writing individualized education plan (IEP) goals.

To be considered socially competent, students must possess a knowledge of socially appropriate behaviors and be able to utilize these behaviors in response to the cues provided by others. The ability of children to use these skills in an appropriate manner, display emotional maturity, and apply problem-solving techniques are critical components of appropriate social interaction.

There are several types of assessments for evaluating a child's social skills. Assessments of social skills for children with Asperger Syndrome should look into not only the extent to which peers may be rejecting this child, but they should also attempt to discover what sort of things the child is doing to contribute to the rejection. The second part, in particular, should include an assessment of possible aggressive, disruptive, withdrawn, and/or socially anxious behaviors. A good assessment should also identify what the child is doing well socially, as these skills can be used as building blocks for teaching new skills. Evaluators should take samples in a variety of environments, with particular attention to those parts of the school day which are nonstructured (recess, lunchtime, etc.) where maximum social interactions are prevalent. Assessments should also take into consideration input and evaluations by the child's parents and teachers. Older students with Asperger Syndrome or high-functioning autism can also help to evaluate their own social skills.

THE COIE AND DODGE METHOD

Recent research indicates that children who have poor peer interactions and/or children who are victimized by peers may experience depression and psychological stress. The development of prosocial skills and empathy may also be inhibited (Coie 1990).

John Coie and Ken Dodge (Coie and Dodge 1983) developed an assessment whereby children from a particular class are individually asked to listen to descriptions of various social behaviors and choose the children in their class who best fit the description by blackening in a bubble beside their names. To administer the test, the evaluator introduces himself to the child and explains that his/her answers will be private, that there are no right or wrong answers, and that this is a way for the evaluator to learn about the children in the class (see Figure 5.1). Children are not told to blacken the bubbles beside their own names if they feel they fit a particular category. Thus, they are not evaluating *themselves.*

Student nomination interview

Beginning the interview

When you sit down, introduce yourself to the child: 'My name is _____. Tell me your name. I'm glad you can help me today. I'm going to ask you some questions about kids in your class. This is not a test – there are no right or wrong answers. I'm just interested in your school and what you think about the kids here. I will keep your answers private – just between you and me. I won't tell the other kids or anyone else what you say. You are being a big help by telling me what you think – because that is one way I'll be able to learn about the kids in your class.'

The interview

1. Now I'm going to ask you which of the kids in your class you like a lot. Tell me the names of the kids in your class that you like. Darken the bubble opposite each name mentioned.
2. Sometimes there are kids in our class that we don't like as well as other kids. Name the kids in your class you don't like very much. Darken the bubble opposite each name mentioned.
3. Some kids start fights, say mean things, and hit other kids. Who are the kids in your class who start fights and say mean things? (Give the child time to name at least three children, but don't force them to name three if they have trouble. If the child is struggling to remember, read him/her the names of his/her classmates.)
4. Some kids are really shy around other kids. They play alone and work alone most of the time. They seem to be afraid to be around other kids. Who are the kids who are shy and act afraid to be around other kids?

5. Some kids are really good to have in your class because they cooperate, help others, and share. They let other kids have a turn. Who are the kids who cooperate, help, and share?

6. Some kids get out of their seats a lot, do strange things, and make a lot of noise. They bother people who are trying to work. Who are the kids who get out of their seats and bother people?

7. Some kids get picked on and teased by other kids. They get hit, or pushed, or called names. Who gets picked on and teased by the other kids?

'Thanks! That was a big help. Remember your answers are just between you and me. I won't tell anyone and you won't have to tell anyone, okay?'

(Note: If a child attempts to blacken too many bubbles with regard to a particular question, explain to the child that you only want the names of the children who do this *a lot*.)

Scoring

The 'liked most' children are listed in item #1.

The 'liked least' children are listed in item #2.

The 'aggressive' children are listed in item #3.

The 'withdrawn' children are listed in item #4.

The 'prosocial' children are listed in item #5.

The 'hyper' children are listed in item #6.

The 'victim' children are listed in item #7.

Children who receive more positive nominations and fewer negative nominations are classified as popular with peers.

Children who receive more negative nominations than positive nominations are considered rejected by peers.

Children who receive few nominations of either kind are designated as neglected.

Those who receive many positive *and* negative nominations are considered controversial.

Finally, figure the average number of positive nominations and the average number of negative nominations from the answers provided (this number is not the same as the average number of students). Children who receive an average number of positive as well as an average number of negative nominations are considered 'average.'

Figure 5.1 Student nomination interview

This instrument serves to identify children who are liked, not liked, aggressive, withdrawn, prosocial, disruptive, or those who may be victims. In this test, children who receive more positive nominations and very few negative nominations are classified as 'popular.' Those children who receive few nominations of either kind are designated 'neglected.' There are also children who receive many positive nominations but also many negative nominations. These children are labeled 'controversial.' Finally, those who receive few positive nominations but many negative ones are classified as 're-jected.' Children are described as 'average' if they receive an average number of positive and negative nominations.

It was later shown that children who were classified as 'rejected' had greater incidences of school problems, delinquency, and mental health disorders (Coie *et al.* 1990). Those children who were 'neglected' also needed careful, individual study, as it was unclear if their social withdrawal may contribute to problems later in life. Children who experience poor socialization skills in middle childhood have higher incidences of low self-esteem and loneliness in adolescence (Rubin and Stewart 1996). Therefore, this test is useful to discover children who fit these descriptions so that socialization help can be provided.

A teacher checklist (see Figure 5.2) was also developed whereby teachers rate students on various statements ranging from 'never true' to 'almost always true.' Thus, teacher's opinions of the social skills of the students can be compared with classmates' opinions.

Unfortunately, children appear to be ostracized for other factors not associated with behaviors including odd appearance and handicaps (Bierman 1993). Also, children who have minority status in the classroom may also have fewer positive nominations and more negative nominations (Coie and Dodge 1982). This scale does not address the degree to which these variables affect evaluation results. It also does not take into account parent opinions or the personal opinions of the child with Asperger Syndrome.

THE SKILLSTREAMING ASSESSMENT OF SOCIAL SKILLS

The Skillstreaming Curriculum (McGinnis and Goldstein 1997) includes a thorough checklist (see Figure 5.3) whereby the teacher is asked to rate a child on each observed social skill by awarding them with a '1' if the child is almost never good at using the skill; a '2' if the child is seldom good at using the skill; a '3' if the child is sometimes good at using the skill; a '4' if the child is often good at using the skill; and a '5' if the child is almost always good at using the skill. The child and the parents also have their own checklists for rating these behaviors using the same method (see Figures 5.4 and 5.5).

The Skillstreaming Checklist is a fairly complete method for obtaining data to develop a social skills curriculum because it includes the observations of several individuals and also identifies those areas with which the student feels he/she could use help. The 'fine-tuning' of each question makes it necessary to evaluate the student in a variety of social settings because certain questions can't be answered unless the child is observed in that setting. For instance, one question in the assessment asks, 'Does the student find something to do when he/she has free time?' This is important when deciding if a child needs social skills intervention and in what areas of his/her social behavior. However, it should be noted that information is not gathered from this assessment from the peers of the child in question.

Teacher checklist

Child's name _____ Teacher's name _____

Child's code # _____ Grade: _____School: _____

Note: For each of the following statements, please circle the number that best applies. Use the following scale to determine the best number.

Circle 1 if this statement is NEVER true of this child

Circle 2 if this statement is RARELY true of this child

Circle 3 if this statement is SOMETIMES true of this child

Circle 4 if this statement is OFTEN true of this child

Circle 5 if this statement is VERY OFTEN true of this child

Circle 6 if this statement is USUALLY true of this child

Circle 7 if this statement is ALMOST ALWAYS true of this child

1.	This child is very good at understanding other people's feelings.	1 2 3 4 5 6 7
2.	This child starts fights with peers.	1 2 3 4 5 6 7
3.	This child is good at games and sports: a good athlete.	1 2 3 4 5 6 7
4.	Other children actively dislike this child and reject him or her from their play.	1 2 3 4 5 6 7
5.	This child is too shy to make friends easily.	1 2 3 4 5 6 7
6.	This child gets angry easily and strikes back when he or she is threatened or teased.	1 2 3 4 5 6 7
7.	Other children like this child and seek him or her out for play.	1 2 3 4 5 6 7
8.	This child has trouble sitting still or concentrating.	1 2 3 4 5 6 7
9.	This child acts stuck up and thinks he or she is better than the other children.	1 2 3 4 5 6 7

10. This child gets teased because of physical appearance.   1 2 3 4 5 6 7

11. This child performs poorly in math.   1 2 3 4 5 6 7

12. This child says mean things to peers, such as teasing or name-calling.   1 2 3 4 5 6 7

13. This child tells other children how things should be done.   1 2 3 4 5 6 7

14. This child has problems with personal hygiene, smells bad, or looks dirty or messy.   1 2 3 4 5 6 7

15. This child makes a lot of comments that are not related to what the group is doing; many of these comments are self-related.   1 2 3 4 5 6 7

16. This child is self-conscious and easily embarrassed.   1 2 3 4 5 6 7

17. This child is a leader, and can tell others what should be done but is not too bossy.   1 2 3 4 5 6 7

18. This child always claims that other children are to blame in a fight and feels that they started the trouble.   1 2 3 4 5 6 7

19. This child complains or whines a lot.   1 2 3 4 5 6 7

20. This child does not stand up for himself or herself when someone picks on him/her.   1 2 3 4 5 6 7

21. This child usually wants to be in charge and set the rules and give orders.   1 2 3 4 5 6 7

22. This child usually plays or works alone.   1 2 3 4 5 6 7

23. This child acts silly or immature.   1 2 3 4 5 6 7

24. This child uses physical force, or threatens to use physical force in order to dominate other kids.   1 2 3 4 5 6 7

25. This child performs poorly in reading.   1 2 3 4 5 6 7

26. This child gets his or her feelings hurt easily.   1 2 3 4 5 6 7

27. This child seeks the teacher's attention too often.   1 2 3 4 5 6 7

28. When a peer accidentally hurts this child (such as by bumping into him/her), this child assumes that the peer meant to do it, and then overreacts with anger and fighting.   1 2 3 4 5 6 7

29. This child is very aware of the effects of his/her behavior on others.   1 2 3 4 5 6 7

30. This child never seems to have a good time.   1 2 3 4 5 6 7

31. This child does things that other children think are strange or inappropriate.   1 2 3 4 5 6 7

32. This child has trouble completing assignments.   1 2 3 4 5 6 7

33. This child threatens or bullies others in order to get his or her own way.   1 2 3 4 5 6 7

34. This child is physically attractive.   1 2 3 4 5 6 7

35. This child makes odd noises or unusual comments.   1 2 3 4 5 6 7

36. This child tries to dominate classmates and pushes self into existing play or work groups.   1 2 3 4 5 6 7

37. This child is timid about joining other children and usually stays just outside the group without joining it.   1 2 3 4 5 6 7

38. This child bothers other kids when they are trying to work.   1 2 3 4 5 6 7

39. This child exaggerates and makes up stories.   1 2 3 4 5 6 7

40. This child gets other kids to gang up on a peer that he or she does not like.   1 2 3 4 5 6 7

41. This child shows off.   1 2 3 4 5 6 7

42. This child is anxious and insecure in social situations.   1 2 3 4 5 6 7

43. This child gets impatient when other children do not do things the way he or she thinks they should be done.   1 2 3 4 5 6 7

44. This child is good to have in a group, shares things, and is helpful.   1 2 3 4 5 6 7

45. This child is frequently absent from school.   1 2 3 4 5 6 7

Figure 5.2 Teacher checklist

THE OBSERVATION PROFILE FOR CHILDREN WITH ASPERGER SYNDROME

The 'Observation Profile' outlined in *Asperger's Syndrome, a Practical Guide for Teachers* (Cumine *et al.* 1998) provides a list of behaviors to observe in the areas of social interaction, social communication,

Teacher/staff skillstreaming checklist

Student: _____ Class/age:_____
Teacher/staff: _____ Date:_____

INSTRUCTIONS: Listed below you will find a number of skills that children are more or less proficient in using. This checklist will help you evaluate how well each child uses the various skills. For each child, rate his/her use of each skill, based on your observation of his/her behavior in various situations.

Circle 1 if the child is *almost never* good at using the skill.

Circle 2 if the child is *seldom* good at using the skill.

Circle 3 is the child is *sometimes* good at using the skill.

Circle 4 if the child is *often* good at using the skill.

Circle 5 if the child is *almost always* good at using the skill.

Please rate the child on all skills listed. If you know of a situation in which the child has particular difficulty in using the skill well, please note it briefly in the space marked 'Problem situation.'

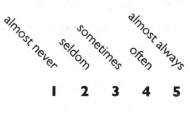

1.   **Listening**: Does the student appear to listen when someone is speaking and make an effort to understand what is said?   1   2   3   4   5

Problem situation:

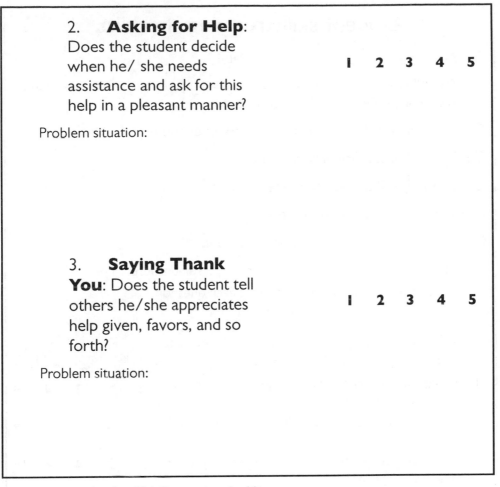

2.   **Asking for Help**: Does the student decide when he/ she needs assistance and ask for this help in a pleasant manner?

1   2   3   4   5

Problem situation:

3.   **Saying Thank You**: Does the student tell others he/she appreciates help given, favors, and so forth?

1   2   3   4   5

Problem situation:

Figure 5.3 Teacher/staff skillstreaming checklist
From Life Lessons for Young Adolescents: An Advisory Guide for Teachers *(1993) by F. Schnempf, S. Freiburg and D. Skadden. Champaign, IL: Research Press.*

social imagination, flexible thinking, motor skills, and organizational skills (see Figure 5.6). With regard to the student's social behaviors, the observer is asked to indicate '1' if there is no cause for concern; '2' mild cause for concern; '3' moderate cause for concern; '4' serious cause for concern; and '5' great cause for concern. As an added benefit, a section is also included for noting what social situations cause the child anxiety, stress, or frustration. In addition, another section is included to help the examiner prioritize the social difficulties which cause him/her the greatest concern. Prior-

Student skillstreaming checklist

Name: _____ Date: _____

INSTRUCTIONS: Each of the questions will ask you about how well you do something. Next to each question is a number.

Circle number 1 if you *almost never* do what the question asks.

Circle number 2 if you *seldom* do it.

Circle number 3 if you *sometimes* do it.

Circle number 4 if you do it *often*.

Circle number 5 if you *almost always* do it.

There are no right or wrong answers to these questions.
Answer the way you really feel about each question.

	almost never	seldom	sometimes	often	almost always
1. Is it easy for me to listen to someone who is talking to me?	1	2	3	4	5
2. Do I ask for help in a friendly way when I need help?	1	2	3	4	5
3. Do I tell people thank you for something they have done for me?	1	2	3	4	5
4. Do I have the materials I need for my classes (like books, pencils, paper)?	1	2	3	4	5
5. Do I understand what to do when directions are given, and do I follow these directions?	1	2	3	4	5
6. Do I finish my schoolwork?	1	2	3	4	5
7. Do I join in on class talks or discussions?	1	2	3	4	5
8. Do I try to help an adult when I think he/she could use the help?	1	2	3	4	5
9. Do I decide what I don't understand about my schoolwork and ask my teacher questions in a friendly way?	1	2	3	4	5
10. It is easy for me to keep doing my schoolwork when people are noisy?	1	2	3	4	5

Figure 5.4 Student skillstreaming checklist

Parent skillstreaming checklist

Name: _____ Date: _____

Child's Name: _____ Birth Date: _____

INSTRUCTIONS: Based on your observations in various situations, rate your child's use of the following skills.

Circle 1 if the child is *almost never* good at using the skill.

Circle 2 if the child is *seldom* good at using the skill.

Circle 3 if the child is *sometimes* good at using the skill.

Circle 4 if the child is *often* good at using the skill.

Circle 5 if the child is *almost always* good at using the skill.

		almost never	seldom	sometimes	often	almost always
1.	**Listening**: Does your child listen when you or others talk to him/her?	1	2	3	4	5
	Comments:					
2.	**Asking for Help**: Does your child decide when he/she needs assistance and ask for this help in a pleasant manner?	1	2	3	4	5
	Comments:					

3.   **Saying Thank You**: Does   1   2   3   4   5
your child tell others he/she
appreciates help given, favors,
and so forth?

　　　Comments:

4.   **Bringing Materials to**   1   2   3   4   5
Class: Does your child
remember the books and
materials he/she needs for
school?

　　　Comments:

Figure 5.5 Parent skillstreaming checklist

itizing input from the observations can certainly make the actual
goal development easier and more appropriate.

　　　When conducting this assessment, care should be taken to
observe the student in a wide variety of settings, particularly those
that are less structured where the number of social interactions are
greatest. The observation form can be completed by teachers as
well as parents. However, the student with Asperger Syndrome and
his/her peers do not have input with this assessment.

Observation Profile

Part I Give a brief 'work picture' of the child within the class, noting positive points as well as difficulties.

Part 2 Observed behaviors

Key: 1 No cause for concern

         2 Mild cause for concern

         3 Moderate cause for concern

         4 Serious cause for concern

         5 Great cause for concern

1. Social interaction	1	2	3	4	5
a) ability to use gesture, body posture, facial expression and eye-to-eye gaze in 1: 1 situation					
b) ability to use gesture, body posture, facial expression and eye-to-eye gaze in group interaction					
c) ability to follow social cues in 1: 1 – with adults					
d) ability to follow social cues in 1: 1 – with other children					
e) ability to follow social cues in group interaction					
f) ability to share an activity with other children					
g) ability to share an activity with an adult					
h) ability to develop peer friendships					

i) ability to seek comfort/affection when upset					
j) ability to offer comfort/affection to others					
k) ability to share in others' enjoyment/pleasure					
l) ability to imitate other children					
m) ability to imitate adults					
n) ability to show different responses to different people in different situations					
o) ability to respond appropriately to social praise					
p) ability to respond appropriately to criticism					

Comments

2. **Social communication**	1	2	3	4	5
a) ability to respond when called by name					
b) ability to follow verbal instructions in 1: 1 setting					
c) ability to follow verbal instructions in a small group setting					
d) ability to follow verbal instructions in a whole class setting					
e) ability to take turns in conversations					
f) ability to initiate conversation					
g) ability to change topic of conversation					
h) ability to maintain an appropriate conversation					
i) ability to show awareness of the listener's needs					

j)	ability to give appropriate nonverbal signals as a listener				
k)	ability to change the topic or style of a conversation to suit the listener				
l)	ability to appropriately change the volume and tone of voice				
m)	ability to recognize and respond to non-verbal clues, e.g. a frown				
n)	ability to understand implied meanings				
o)	ability to tell or write an imaginative story				
p)	ability to relate a sequence of events				
q)	ability to give a simple sequence of instructions				

Comments

3. **Social imagination and flexible thinking**	1	2	3	4	5
a) ability to have varied interests					
b) ability to share interests					
c) ability to change behavior according to the situation					
d) ability to accept changes in rules, routines, or procedures					
e) ability to play imaginatively when alone					
f) ability to play imaginatively together with others					
g) ability to accept others' points of view					
h) ability to generalize learning					

i) ability to transfer skills across the curriculum					
j) ability to plan an event or a task					
k) ability to suggest possible explanations for events					
l) ability to use inference and deduction					

Comments

4. Motor and organizational skills	1	2	3	4	5
a) ability to find his way around the classroom					
b) ability to find his way around the school					
c) ability to sit still					
d) ability to sit amongst a small group					
e) ability to sit amongst a large group, e.g. in assembly					
f) ability to find and organize the equipment he needs for a given task					
g) ability to write legibly and draw accurately					
h) ability to get changed without help, e.g. for PE					
i) ability to organize his movements in PE and Games					

Comments

Note the settings in which the child shows anxiety, stress, or frustration.
Eg: PE in the Hall / at transition times / sitting amongst a large group.

Prioritize the 3 difficulties which cause you the greatest concern
1.
2.
3.

Figure 5.6 Observation Profile

THE WALKER SOCIAL SKILLS ASSESSMENT

The 'Walker Social Skills Curriculum: The Accepts Program' (Walker, McConnell 1988) consists of a 'placement' test to evaluate social skills. Teachers are given rating instructions on a scale and asked to evaluate classroom skills, basic interaction skills, making friends skills, coping skills, and getting along skills as a placement along a continuum.

Although this test does attempt to measure social skills in a variety of social settings, it does not take into account student, peer, or parent perceptions of those skills. However, the assessment could be utilized by a parent, but the questions may not be completely appropriate; for instance: 'The student follows the established classroom rules.'

Accepts placement test

Teacher rating instructions

Please read each statement on the placement test carefully and circle the corresponding number that is descriptive/representative of the child's behavior. The numbers 1–5 are a *continuous* scale. Circling number 1 indicates that the statement is *not* descriptive or true; circling number 3 states that the statement is *moderately* descriptive or true of the child; and circling number 5 indicates it is *very* descriptive or true of the child.

For example, an item might read as follows:

The student shares laughter with classmates

Not descriptive or true	Moderately descriptive or true	Very descriptive or true
1 2	3 4	5

If you feel the child does *not* share laughter with classmates, then by circling number 1 you would indicate that the statement is not descriptive or true of that child.

If you feel that the child does this *some* of the time, then by circling number 3 you would indicate that the statement is *moderately* descriptive or true.

If you feel that this happens most of the time, then by circling number 5 you would indicate that the statement is *very* descriptive or true of the child. Otherwise, circle the number (2 or 4) that most closely indicates your rating of the item.

Area I: Classroom skills	Not descriptive or true	Moderately descriptive or true	Very descriptive or true		
1. The student sits quietly and pays attention to what the teacher is saying.	1	2	3	4	5
2. When the teacher tells the student to do something, the student does it.	1	2	3	4	5
3. The student produces work of acceptable quality.	1	2	3	4	5
4. The student follows the established classroom rules.	1	2	3	4	5

Area II: Basic interaction skills

1. The student maintains eye contact while speaking or when spoken to.	1	2	3	4	5
2. The student speaks in a moderate tone of voice (neither too loud/too soft).	1	2	3	4	5
3. The student seeks out others to interact with and initiates a conversation.	1	2	3	4	5
4. The student pays attention when spoken to.	1	2	3	4	5
5. The student responds/answers when spoken to.	1	2	3	4	5
6. The student converses by saying things which are relevant to the topic.	1	2	3	4	5
7. The student shares a conversation by speaking for about the same amount of time as they listen.	1	2	3	4	5
8. The student asks questions that request information about someone/something.	1	2	3	4	5
9. The student keeps a conversation going.	1	2	3	4	5

Area III: Getting along skills

1. The student uses polite words such as 'please,' 'thank you,' and 'excuse me.'	1	2	3	4	5

Figure 5.7 Accepts placement test: Teacher rating intructions

In conclusion, social skills assessments need to consist of the following characteristics to be effective in teasing out social weaknesses in children with Asperger Syndrome:

1. Assessments need to be measurable: they need to be defined in terms that indicate the degree of need for instruction in particular social areas.

2. They should allow for teachers (regular and special education) to share their input. Sometimes it is useful to obtain data from observations where teachers not familiar with the child also have the ability to share their impressions (for instance, a recess monitor or a cafeteria monitor).

3. Assessments should be easy enough to administer so that a variety of individuals familiar with the child can offer their observation input.

4. Assessments of social behavior should take place across several days in a variety of social settings and not be limited to one sampling. This author once participated in an IEP team meeting where the principal shared results of an assessment she had completed for a child with Asperger Syndrome. The assessment was completed by observation of the child during quiet time in reading. There was no interaction required with his peers during this particular sampling. The principal reported that the child exhibited no behavior problems, and the district was finding him ineligible for social skills instruction!

5. The child's parents should be able to provide information because they observe the child's interactions at many social activities outside the structured school environment.

6.   The older child with Asperger Syndrome should also be able to offer his/her perceptions of and feelings about his/her peer relations.

7.   It may be that the child with Asperger Syndrome has information-processing difficulties which may be interfering with his/her perceptions of what is actually going on in his/her peer group. Therefore, obtaining peer input is also useful.

8.   Finally, the goal of all social skills assessments should be to obtain an accurate account of what areas are causing the *most* concern for the child so that meaningful, individualized, measurable and developmentally appropriate goals can be written to address these deficits.

CHAPTER SIX

Interventions to Promote Acquisition

'There was a child went forth each day,
And the first object he look'd upon, that object he became
And that object became part of him for the day
or a certain part of the day,
Or for many years or stretching cycles of years...'

– Walt Whitman

Currently, there exists a small variety of social skills curriculums that teachers can use to assist children with Asperger Syndrome and high-functioning autism to encourage development of their social skills. Each of these has advantages and disadvantages. There also exists some excellent research that offers us some practical ways to introduce social skills in mainstream education. This research, coupled with the suggestions of experienced teachers who work with these children, will be provided in this chapter.

I. THE CIRCLE OF FRIENDS PROGRAM

The Circle of Friends program has been successfully used with typical children who have a child with a disability in their classroom (Forest *et al.* 1993). The main purpose of the Circle of Friends program is to take the burden of making friendships off the individual who has a handicap in this area and encourage their classroom peers to learn to value the child with the disability and initiate friendships with him/her. This program can be adapted to suit elementary-age children as well as older students. It is also particularly helpful when teasing is occurring. If some peers begin to develop relationships with the child who has a disability, this will encourage them to 'stick-up' for these kids and help to prevent future harassment. It will also prevent the child with autism from being alone and vulnerable to such attacks.

First, an individual with a good grasp of the child's disability and his/her shortcomings gives a brief description of what Asperger Syndrome is and the symptoms that the student has at this time. Including a project where the children can 'step into the shoes' of the child with the disability and learn what it feels like to have this disorder is particularly useful. For instance, when discussing the hearing sensitivities of these children, it may be useful to have several children hold a loud conversation in one area of the room. At the same time, play a loud radio adjusting the volume up and down, ring a bell occasionally, etc., to create an environment where filtering out background noises and understanding what is being discussed becomes extremely difficult. The instructor should make sure that the presentation is given to those students who currently interact with the child and also in age-appropriate language. Children who are causing problems for the student with Asperger Syndrome should be required to attend the presentation so that they may learn to be more sympathetic towards the student with this disability. The presenter may also field questions about the disability.

Next, an overhead projector can be used to illustrate how typical children and adults have 'circles' of friends and acquaintances, the teacher drawing the circles as he/she explains them to his/her audience.

Figure 6.1 Circles of friends

As individuals, to be emotionally healthy, we need to have several concentric 'circles' of people to interact with. The first innermost circle contains those people who are our immediate family members. The next circle contains those people who are our extended family members, followed by one which would contain our close friends. The next circle would represent acquaintances or other peer relationships with whom there is interaction (classmates, neighbors). Then a circle would be drawn which includes those individuals who are paid to interact with us (e.g. teachers, coaches, doctors). Lastly, the outermost circle includes those individuals we interact with in society who do not need to know us personally (e.g. bank tellers, postmen, firemen).

The instructor then draws the concentric circles that illustrate the present condition of the individual with autism. He/she then makes a direct request for individuals to volunteer to help fill in the circles. Preferably, an overhead depicting specifically how this can occur will be included:

- sitting with the individual on the bus and encouraging conversation

- sitting with the individual at lunch and doing the same

- meeting the individual at a school dance

- attending a football game with the individual

- walking home with him/her

- spending recess with the student.

It is important to emphasize that the individual with autism will need respect and understanding. The instructor will be appealing to the students' sense of fairness and kindness – explaining that the individual has a disability that prevents him/her from being successful at these things. Several peers can volunteer to 'take turns' at the above, or do them together. An adult will be assigned to monitor the program, troubleshoot problems with peers, and encourage feedback in later meetings.

To summarize, the main benefits or advantages of this program are that:

1. It provides answers for those who have trouble understanding the handicapped individual's behavior.

2. It takes the burden off the individual with the social handicap to make friends.

3. It promotes acceptance, understanding, and tolerance of individuals with disabilities.

4. It may reduce teasing and scape-goating.

5. It provides typical students with an awareness of individuals with disabilities and a chance to develop friendships based on mutual respect and concern for others.

The disadvantages of such a program are that:

1. It may produce embarrassment for the individual with the disability; one should weigh this disadvantage with the effect that teasing and isolation may be having upon the child.

2. There may be a loss of privacy for the individual with the disability.

3. Proper planning needs to be done to ensure the success of the project; an adult will need to monitor the project's progress and continue to set up peer supporters.

4. Peer training will need to be provided.

5. It may become a burden for some typical children. Frequent teacher contact with volunteer peers should be encouraged so that these children do not feel 'guilty' if they want to relinquish their turns or if they no longer want to participate in the project.

II. USE OF THE CHILD'S STRENGTHS, TALENTS, AND 'PASSIONS' TO PROMOTE INTERACTION

Mr. William Stillman, who works for the Department of Public Welfare in Pennsylvania, describes his passion for the *Wizard of Oz*. He is a foremost expert on the subject and has coauthored several books. He explains that he prefers the use of the word 'passion' to 'obsession' because he believes that it has a better and less clinical connotation.

As a child, Mr. Stillman was frequently forced in math class to count bundles of dowels in 'sets', which he described as completely meaningless and frustrating for him. He detested those frequent math tests doing just that, which he feels contributed to his poor grades in math. He tells parents and teachers that if one of his teachers had used his passion for the *Wizard of Oz* to teach math (for instance, counting yellow bricks from the yellow brick road), he knows he would have grasped the concept quickly and happily.

Research has shown this to be true with social skills as well! Passions can be tremendous motivators for encouraging appropriate social behavior.

> Focusing on strengths also taps areas that are motivating to individuals with autism. Finding motivators of children with autism is both challenging and critical. The challenge is that children with autism may be unresponsive to typical motivators such as praise, play opportunities, or foods. Yet, motivators are essential for behavioral change and for learning. The activities that interest the child with Asperger Syndrome should be explored and incorporated in interventions for that child. (McAllister *et al.* 1996, p.3)

In one study (Charlop-Christy and Haymes 1996), children with autism who had obsessions were encouraged to use them as reinforcers. In this study, child #1 had a fixation with globes and maps; child #2 had an interest in paste caps and coffee swizzle sticks;

child #3 enjoyed plastic toy helicopters and a specific family photo album; and child #4 enjoyed a variety of balls and balloons. The children then participated in a range of educational tasks, using the obsessions as reinforcers for good behavior. 'For all the children, both the obsession-only and obsession-plus reductive procedures conditions were the most effective in decreasing the inappropriate behaviors' (Charlop-Christy and Haymes 1996, p.536).

In another study (Baker *et al.* 1998) the obsessions of young autistic children were used to design play activities and games, including a game of tag played with a giant map of the United States for a child with Asperger Syndrome who was fascinated with US geography, and a follow-the-leader game with Disney items for a child fascinated by Disney figures.

If the teacher offers praise to a student with Asperger Syndrome and finds that this is not meaningful to him/her, the teacher should do some exploration into discovering the student's own motivators and include these in his/her education program. He or she should encourage the use of these 'passions' in a variety of social skills activities.

EXAMPLE I

A fourth-grade student with Asperger Syndrome is an expert in computers. The teacher used the child to 'trouble-shoot' all computer questions that other students had in class and allowed him/her to be excused from the assignment at-hand to do this. The child with Asperger Syndrome smiled brightly in response to helping his fifth classmate and said, 'Everybody needs my help!'

EXAMPLE II

One child has an all-encompassing desire to read about, collect, and design stories involving Beanie Babies. His teacher devised a Beanie Baby game for recess. Since this child was the 'star,' all children wanted him on their team, thus encouraging the development of the child's self-esteem.

One should never underestimate the power that using these motivators will have on children with Asperger Syndrome. Many teachers are thoroughly amazed at what these children will do when their 'passions' are utilized in this way! A creative teacher can certainly take whatever talent, passion, or obsession the child has and use it as a tool for promoting successful social interaction. Parents can also provide wonderful information about what types of things motivate and interest their children, and these contributions should certainly be valued.

Some applied behavioral analysis (ABA) treatment programs have adopted the goal that the obsessions of children with high-functioning autism should be 'extinguished.' However, extinguishing these behaviors may also eliminate ways to foster appropriate social interaction. If these obsessions are preventing the individual's ability to participate in more natural activities with peers, they can be limited in duration by teachers and can serve as rewards for appropriate behavior without emotional upheaval.

EXAMPLE III
One teacher knew that a child with high-functioning autism loved to read hardware magazines, and if left to his own devices, would do this for hours on end. The child was rewarded with 15 minutes of 'magazine' time when he successfully participated in recess without being aggressive with his classmates.

The advantages of using 'passions' in the classroom include:

1. An increase in self-esteem for the child with Asperger Syndrome.

2. Peers learn to value and respect the child's talents.

3. 'Passions' are a highly motivating way to encourage social skills instruction.

4. 'Passions' can be a positive way to manage difficult behaviors and encourage appropriate ones.

The disadvantages of their use may include:

1. The need for advanced planning and creativity on the part of the teacher.

2. Required knowledge of the interests and motivators of the child.

3. The need for continual teacher monitoring to make sure that incorporating the 'passion' is having the desired effect.

III. USE OF VIDEOTAPE

Many individuals with Asperger Syndrome learn from visual presentations rather than auditory ones. They need to 'see' what they are trying to learn, either through written words or pictures. Frequently, the use of videotape can provide a wonderful learning experience for children with this diagnosis.

In her training sessions, Carol Gray, a Jenison Public Schools consultant in Michigan, describes Eric, a teenage student with high-functioning autism, as the impetus that helped her to develop her 'social stories' concept (Gray 1996; see page 135). Eric, who was mainstreamed into some regular education classes, frequently interrupted the teacher with meaningless questions. All previous attempts to eliminate this behavior were unsuccessful. Eventually, Eric interrupted a speaker in the auditorium during an assembly, which evoked much laughter from his peers. He was not aware that they were laughing at him and assumed they were laughing at the speaker. Ms. Gray used a videotape of the assembly to teach Eric why he was being disrespectful. Eric finally understood why interrupting was not appropriate, and this resulted in a complete change of his behavior.

Other parents have also used videotapes from soap operas to teach individuals with autism to read facial expressions, learn about empathy, and to study other social rules of conduct.

EXAMPLE I

One parent used the popular TV shows *Third Rock from the Sun, Mr. Bean* and *Seinfeld* because they are filled with illustrations that can be used to teach appropriate social behavior. The episodes were taped and then reviewed with their child. These shows frequently demonstrate *inappropriate* behaviors and the characters get into considerable trouble because of their poor social skills. The parents used these tapes to teach what *not* to do in certain social situations.

In another study (Charlop and Milstein 1989) adults recorded a conversation on videotape as they conversed about toys, in particular toys of interest to the children who would watch the tape. Later, the children watched the tape several times. The therapist instructed the children to 'do the same' as the video and handed the children toys. They were praised if they were able to duplicate the video. Charlop and Milstein found that, later, the children were able to use their new-found conversation skills successfully in settings with others.

Advantages of using videotape to teach social skills include:

1. The use of visual learning (a strength for many children with Asperger Syndrome), which can be combined easily with auditory instruction.

2. The ability to rewind and fast-forward, which can be very effective for studying or reviewing a social skill.

3. Because of the tendency for these children to have excellent rote memory, they are able to repeat back what they see and hear with ease.

The disadvantages may include:

1. Generalization of the skill may still be difficult.

2. Audiovisual equipment needs to be regularly available.

IV. ENVIRONMENTAL MANIPULATIONS

The LEAP Preschool, a program of the Watson Institute, an approved private school in a western suburb of Pittsburgh, Pennsylvania, provides instruction for preschool children with autism in an inclusive setting. This program offers a typical classroom environment to four children with autism and eight typically developing children per classroom. The program is designed so that children with autism can learn to imitate and model from typical peers. Every moment the child with high-functioning autism spends in the classroom is designed to increase and maximize appropriate peer interactions.

EXAMPLE I

During an art project, not every child gets a pair of scissors – these are distributed so that children with autism must request them from peers and share them with others. At snack time, the student may not be given juice. If the student wants juice, he/she must ask for it or use a picture card to communicate his/her desire.

EXAMPLE II

Arranging the environment to incorporate 'surprise' is sometimes useful to encourage social interaction. For instance, the child goes to the cabinet where glue is usually found. One day, however, instead of glue, he finds a stuffed animal. Or, when he opens a tube of potato chips, he finds popcorn. The element of 'surprise' will often initiate communication.

Camp WISP, another product of the Watson Institute, was developed by Dr. Joseph McAllister and Dr. Karleen Preator as a summer program for including children with high-functioning autism with typical children in neighborhood summer camps. This program is a natural extension of the school year. Children with Asperger Syndrome attend these camps with therapeutic support staff trained in the social deficits of these children. Individual social goals are written for the children and staff monitor and keep data to show that they are making progress towards meeting their goals. They also help to facilitate social interaction with typical peers.

Dr. Joseph McAllister and Dr. Karleen Preator describe that even the 'swimming time' portion of the day and the seating arrangements at lunch are pre-planned to promote maximum interaction. [Author's note: teachers should remember the sensory impairments these children may have, as discussed in Chapter 4. If a child with autism can not tolerate having his/her personal space invaded, choosing a lunch partner who is 'all over the place' will cause extreme stress for him/her. If he/she is too distraught with sensory issues, a planned seating arrangement at lunch may not have much benefit.]

Children with autism at Camp WISP are also provided with personal grease boards to help staff use pictures and words to encourage social communication with peers. An unplanned benefit of using these grease boards resulted when staff reported that they were 'kid magnets.' Typical children began to use them with the children with high-functioning autism, playing games and interacting as they would with other peers.

V. USE OF SOCIAL SCRIPTS

Carol Gray has also developed a concept called 'Social Comic Strips' whereby proper social behavior is illustrated visually with comic strips (Gray 1994). This method has proven to be very successful because the learning is visual (a strength for many children with autism) and because learning is broken down into 'frames' or small parts.

One does not have to be an expert in art to utilize this method. Stick figures with or without 'conversation balloons' are just as acceptable.

EXAMPLE I

David, a twelve-year-old child with high-functioning autism, frequently interrupted family members who were having conversations with other family members. His father devised a comic strip for him to help him learn when it was appropriate to initiate conversation:

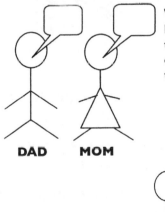

Figure 6.2 Adapted from Comic Strips Conversation, Carol Gray, Future Horizons, Arlington, Texas 1994

The advantages of the comic strips method include:

1. Visual learning, a strength for many children with autism.

2. High interest in the comic strips.

3. Learning is broken down into manageable 'chunks'.

4. The strips can be stored in a book and referred to often for rehearsal.

5. The comic strips provide for rote memorization of social skills.

The disadvantages include:

1. The need for reasonable drawing ability.

2. The difficulty of including exceptions to rules of social behavior in the strips.

VI. CREATING SOCIAL LANGUAGE GROUPS

Speech therapy is offered for children with language acquisition or pronunciation problems in elementary school. As mentioned previously, children with pragmatic language problems (social language deficits) are frequently not identified as being in need of services. However, pragmatic difficulties can be just as hampering to the student as other types of language delays. Addressing these weak areas can be accomplished in social language groups with typical peers. Notes can be sent home with children who possess good pragmatic language (or social skills) asking parents to give permission for these children to serve as peer models for other children who need help acquiring these skills. A pull-out session once or twice a week can be used to introduce social skills lessons that will benefit not only the child with Asperger Syndrome, but also children who are painfully shy, those who are not adjusting well socially, and children who may be identified as class bullies. The group should contain enough children with good pragmatic skills for the child with Asperger Syndrome to model from and practice with.

Advantages of using this method of instruction are:

1. It provides hands-on practice for the child with Asperger Syndrome.

2. The environment can be manipulated to provide success for the child.

3. All children can learn about and work on improving proper social behavior.

4. Deficits of children with Asperger Syndrome can be discovered and addressed as the teacher is able to watch his/her social interactions more closely with typical peers.

5. It provides a way to introduce a social skill and practice it in small group settings where the skill can be monitored and strengthened before it is used in large groups or more generalized interactions.

The disadvantages of using social language groups include:

1. The possibility that some parents of typical children may object to the pull-out session. Pull-outs need to be structured during activities where children are not losing instructional time and only after parents have given permission.

2. There may be potential embarrassment for the child with Asperger Syndrome if he/she is not able to complete the

goals of the lesson. Teachers should be aware of this and plan for some success with each lesson.

VI. THE SKILLSTREAMING CURRICULUM

As mentioned previously in Chapter 5, the Skillstreaming program was developed by Ellen McGinnis and Arnold Goldstein (McGinnis and Goldstein 1997). It consists of an early child, an elementary student, and an adolescent curriculum. There are several parts to each curriculum.

The first part of the Skillstreaming Curriculum consists of the individual social skills, broken down into easy-to-follow steps in manual form for the student and the teacher.

The second part consists of program forms which include the assessment tests; student handouts; teacher, parent, and student checklists; homework reports; and parent/teacher skill-rating forms. The third part of the curriculum contains 'skill cards' for student use which list behavior steps for the student to follow when mastering each individual social skill. For instructors who want a quick overview of the curriculum, a videotape is also available.

Skillstreaming is particularly helpful because it identifies specific target social goals and provides a way to address them through the use of a lesson plan. It utilizes a seamless approach because the instruction to develop a specific goal continues from school to home. The homework reports allow the student to generalize the social skill taught at school by trying it out in a home environment and reporting back to the teacher. There are also school-to-home note forms where teachers can request that parents implement a homework assignment with the student. Forms are included to rate the student in group settings and to allow for rating by both the parent and the teacher. A bonus feature are the

Skill 39: Avoiding trouble

STEPS

1. Stop and think about what the consequences of an action might be.
2. Decide if you want to stay out of trouble.
3. Decide what to tell the other person.
4. Tell the person.

NOTES FOR DISCUSSION

With students, create a list of the possible consequences of particular actions.

Discuss how to decide if it is important to avoid these consequences.

Discuss how to say no in a friendly but firm way.

SUGGESTED SITUATIONS

School: Another student wants you to help him/her cheat on a test.

Home: Your brother or sister wants you to take money from your parents.

Peer group: A friend wants you to tease another friend.

COMMENTS

It is important to teach students to anticipate the consequences of their actions. They may still choose to accept the consequences.

(From 'Life Lessons for Young Adolescents: An Advisory Guide for Teachers' p. 129 by F. Schrumpf, S. Freiburg, and D. Skadden. Champaign, IL: Research Press. Copyright 1993 by the authors. Reprinted by permission.)

Figure 6.3 Skill 39: Avoiding trouble

'achievement' award certificates that can be provided to the students who master their goals.

The advantages of the program are:

1. It provides clear identification of problem areas for the student.

2. It encourages active involvement of the parent and student in identifying weak areas of social development.

3. It provides a seamless approach of instruction from home to school.

4. It offers specific ways to target social goals.

5. It is age-appropriate – little adaptation is needed. However, the elementary school program may need to be combined with the preschool program for students who are younger or lagging behind in their elementary-age social skills.

The following concerns have been expressed about the program:

1. To be most effective for the student, the teacher will need to be willing to adopt a 'team' approach with the student and the student's parents.

2. There is some preparation time required in learning the curriculum and how it is to be used.

VII. SOCIAL STORIES

'Social Stories' describes the program developed by Carol Gray for teaching social skills to children with autism (Gray 1994). One particular social skill is addressed in each story. The stories consist of four types of sentences: descriptive, directive, perspective, and control.

- **Descriptive sentences** explain what occurs and why, who is involved, and provide the background for the story. They state basic information.

- **Directive sentences** provide direction to the child. They instruct the student on how to do something or how to respond. They frequently use the words 'I can' or 'I will'. They are never written using negative words such as 'I will not' or 'I won't.'

- **Perspective sentences** describe the reactions of other people and their feelings. These sentences are a great way to instruct the student in how it feels to 'step into the shoes' of another.

- **Control sentences** are sometimes written by the student to help him recall information.

The writer of a social story should use between three and five of every other type of sentence for every one directive type. He/she should also use first-person present tense, the vocabulary and comprehension level of the student, address one social skill per story, and keep the story as brief as possible.

Figure 6.4 is an example of a social story written for a boy who fears Halloween parties at school because of the masks and scary costumes. The types of sentences are written for explanation purposes only and should not be included for the student.

Social stories address the difficulty that children with high-functioning autism have in 'reading minds.' This is commonly referred to as the 'theory of mind' deficit. Children with Asperger Syndrome, as we discussed before, have difficulty thinking about the thoughts of others and granting them importance. It also makes it difficult for these individuals to see that the things that happen to them may be accidental and not intentional. They have difficulty seeing the whole picture, rather than just the details.

The advantages of the social stories method include:

1. Social stories help to correct false assumptions or 'rigid' thinking.

'Halloween'

Donna Baughman, Itinerate Teacher,
Westmoreland Intermediate Unit,
Greensburg, Pennsylvania

Halloween is October 31st.	(Descriptive)
On Halloween, many of us will dress in costumes and go trick-or-treating.	(Descriptive)
We will get lots of candy and other goodies from our neighbors.	(Descriptive)
In school, we will have Halloween parties. Some sixth graders may dress-up in scary costumes and masks. They may make funny noises and monster movements. They may touch me.	(Descriptive)
This really frightens me and makes me nervous!	(Perspective)
It's okay to feel this way!	(Perspective)
I know they will not hurt me. They are only acting: just like in the movies.	(Descriptive)
If I feel scared, I will take a deep breath and remember that those monsters are really my friends.	(Directive)
The masks are plastic and rubber. Once the masks come off, I will see their faces.	(Descriptive)
I can enjoy my Halloween celebration in school.	(Directive)
I am with my friends.	(Descriptive)

Figure 6.4 'Halloween'

2. Social stories provide a 'formula' to teach a social skill.

3. This method uses a visual medium (a strength for many of these children).

4. Social stories help to teach 'theory of mind' skills.

5. They can be utilized by teachers and parents across many environments.

6. Social stories can be saved and reviewed as needed.

The disadvantages of using this method include:

1. One must put careful thought into writing the social story according to the formula.

2. The social story might not be able to address 'exceptions' to the rules of social behavior – an important consideration for children who are very literal in their thinking.

3. Some training is required for the writer to use this method correctly.

VIII. TEACH GAME-PLAYING SKILLS

In order for children to be able to enter into social activities, they must understand the rules of games that children commonly play. Parents often do not include the child in neighborhood outdoor baseball, soccer, basketball, etc., leagues because they feel that the child will hurt himself/herself or because they are not good at these sports and they may be teased, further damaging their self-esteem. However, if the children are not taught the rules of these games, not only will they be isolated from their peers who are participating in teams and leagues, they will also be isolated from peer play in the neighborhood and at school. Parents and teachers should at least make an effort to teach the child minimal skills required to participate in these games so that their children will not be further excluded from their peers.

Parents and teachers should also make an effort to teach children games that are age-appropriate to play indoors as well (i.e.

checkers, chess, etc.). Even basic game-playing skills such as twirling a spinner, moving a game piece, rolling a die, or removing cards from the top of a deck, may need to be taught first. Providing children who have Asperger Syndrome with 'kid magnets,' as previously explained, can also increase the opportunities for social interaction. One mother makes a point of buying her child the 'latest craze' video games and invites neighborhood children over for play dates on a rotating basis. The typical children enjoy opportunities to use the games and activities, and the child with Asperger Syndrome gets additional social skills practice.

Additionally, it would be practical and more useful if the child with Asperger Syndrome could learn the game-playing skills needed *prior* to playing the game with peers. It may be too much effort for the child with Asperger Syndrome to learn and use game-playing skills in addition to practicing appropriate social skills.

IX. USE OF PEERS FOR PROMPTING, MODELING, OR COACHING

Peers can be valuable coaches to children with Asperger Syndrome or high-functioning autism. They can be used in several ways including:

- recess companions
- bus companions
- peer tutors
- physical education partners
- computer buddies
- lunch-time partners
- after-school friends
- homework companions.

Peers can provide guidance, instruction, encouragement, assistance, and accompaniment. They offer valuable insights into the social arenas of children to which adults do not have access. Peers can serve as 'prompters' or 'reinforcers' for the children with disabilities. A study was conducted and reported on the effects of modeling and coaching on the interactions of kindergarten children with their peers who have autism (Handlan and Bloom 1993). The purpose of the study was to determine if, given proper instruction, prompting, modeling, and coaching of peers would increase the interactions of typical children with children who have autism. At game tables, teachers instructed typical students to model and coach children with autism while using game-playing skills such as rolling the die, initiating a turn, operating game pieces, and moving a marker. 'Verbal reinforcement was modeled using specific praise and the child's name. For example, the teacher would say, "Good job, Joey. You waited for your turn." Prompting consisted, for example, of a typical student saying, "Remember to wait your turn, Joey"' (Handlan and Bloom 1993, p.3). The teachers would also coach the students as to when would be a good time to prompt. Results of the study show the greatest increase in interactions between each typical child and the child with autism occurred during the modeling and coaching phase. However, some children also continued this practice into the educational curriculum, the cafeteria, and the playground.

In addition to the benefits of increased interaction during school, positive outcomes were also observed outside the school. Several incidents were reported where children initiated interaction in public places with the children with autism. Also, a few parents of the typical children phoned the school to report their pleasure at having their child participate in such a project. 'Finally, the kindergarten teacher requested that other students be mainstreamed in her class the next year and became an advocate for other inclusion efforts in the school' (Handlan and Bloom 1993, p.7).

Peer tutors should be carefully chosen, and the child with Asperger Syndrome should have a say in this if possible. Choosing a peer who has a high approval rating with his/her classmates often reduces the amount of teasing that the child with Asperger Syndrome may have to tolerate because of the peer's ability to thwart such activity for him/her. Also, it is important to praise and reward peers for the important work they are doing for a child with a disability.

There is a lesson to be learned: 'The results of this study strongly point to the need for structuring the environment to ensure success in mainstreaming for both nondisabled children and children with autism. Opportunities must be provided for typical children to learn how to play with children with autism' (Handlan and Bloom 1993, p.7). Interactions will most likely not work if typical peers are not trained in how to approach the child, how to keep him/her engaged with cues and prompts, and what sort of activities to try that the child with Asperger Syndrome will most enjoy. Regular education teachers will not be able to accomplish this without help and consultation from special education staff. Videotape trainings for teachers are useful. Special education programs at local colleges which could provide trained volunteers may also be helpful.

Studies have shown that when teachers are provided with the supports they need and experience success with inclusion, they begin to lose their fear of it.

X. PREPARATION FOR TRANSITION

Children with Asperger Syndrome and high-functioning autism generally have difficulty with changes in their routine and environment. Disruptions in their schedules may make them distraught. It will then be extremely difficult for them to display appropriate social interactions. Teachers can assist with planning for transitions in several ways. It should be emphasized that many difficult behaviors can be eliminated by attention to this one area. The devices used to prepare a student with Asperger Syndrome for change are called 'transition devices' or 'transition services'. They enable the student to move from one familiar area or situation to a new one during his/her day. They are as follows:

Activity schedules

Linda Hodgon (Hodgon 1998) and Lynn McClannahan (McClannahan 1999) devote much attention to development of these tools. Activity schedules outline for the student the order of events for the day. Schedules encourage students to become independent and better prepared to move through the day's agenda. The most important advantage of using these tools is that they provide a visual medium for understanding.

One instructor designed a felt-board with moveable time slots and subjects such as math, reading, and music that could be arranged daily for the student in the order they would occur. Changes to the schedule were marked with a big 'lightning bolt.' For instance, if there was going to be a substitute teacher, a lightning bolt was used to designate to the student that this was going to happen in his music class.

Schedules can also be developed by using a corner of the chalkboard or a 3 x 5 card placed unobtrusively on the student's desk. They can be done entirely with pictures, photos, words, objects, or a combination of the above.

Calendars can also be used as schedules.

Often, the use of schedules is criticized by people who claim that they may make the child too dependent on these devices. However,

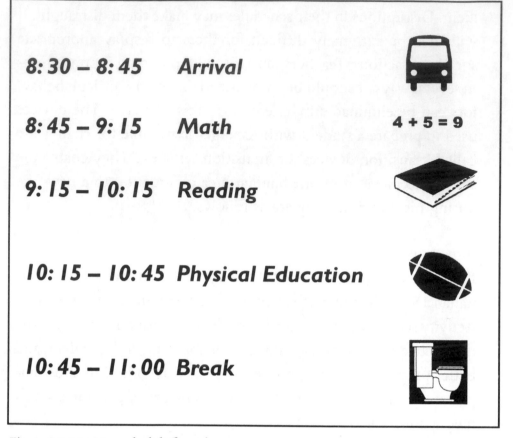

Figure 6.5 Morning schedule for today

this should not be considered a valid argument. Many individuals, adults and children, use various types of activity schedules in daily life to keep organized in busy times. Taking them away because they may become too dependent on them is simply ridiculous, especially if they are working.

For teachers who do not feel as if they are particularly artistic, there exists on the market a software program that produces labels and pictures for a variety of uses. 'Eye-cons' are a product line of Kidaccess, a company founded by computer software engineer, Dr. Jill Lehman (Lehman 1998). Dr. Lehman has developed a product to allow for communication through the use of visual pictures which can be paired with words. Kidaccess will design a cus-

Monday	Tuesday	Wednesday	Thursday	Friday
♫	🖌	🏀	💻	🔬

Figure 6.6 Weekday activities

tom-made set of eye-cons to a teacher's specifications, or provide software for the user to download eye-cons already developed for classroom use. The software is completely compatible with a wide variety of computer programs and is particularly helpful to children who respond well to visual methods of instruction. Eye-cons can be created using a variety of colors and styles. Figure 6.7 is an 'eye-con' for helping a child learn to line up properly in a waiting line.

Mini-schedules

Mini-schedules are written to allow the student to follow the steps on what needs to be done socially within one time-slot (usually an unstructured time of the day, such as the first few minutes when the student arrives at school, or when he/she is waiting in line for transition to the next activity). In this way, children can learn to self-regulate their own behavior in times of the day when it is difficult to have a planned agenda. Teachers can refer the child discreetly to his/her mini-schedule when he/she is looking lost, or is unable to make the adjustment.

Figure 6.7 'Eye-con' for waiting in line
Copyright © 1999 KidAccess, Inc., reprinted with permission

Parent involvement

Parents of children with Asperger Syndrome or high-functioning autism are often experts at preparing their children for change because they have had to do this many times to avoid problems! When a teacher provides the parent with advance notice concerning changes to the child's routine (the cancellation of a field trip or a special class, the absence of the teacher, etc.), the transition planning can begin at home before the child even arrives in school.

'Walking' through a change

Frequently, it is of benefit to the child and teacher actually to practice the change in routine before it happens. Practicing a fire drill, allowing the student to tour his/her classroom the week before school opens, allowing him/her to examine a new textbook before it is used, rehearsing the bathroom procedure – all of these can add to the student's confidence in being able to handle the transition and manage his/her behaviors. Some children will need this preparation for only major changes. Others will need it for such simple changes as a new bulletin board display.

1. I wait quietly in line.

2. I pay for my lunch.

3. I select my food.

4. I sit down.

Figure 6.8 What I do in the cafeteria

Giving five-minute warnings

Providing the child with Asperger Syndrome some 'get ready time' before the change in schedule by giving a five- or ten-minute warning is extremely helpful. For instance, informing the students out loud, 'We are going to go to art class in ten minutes. You will need to put your toys away in five minutes.' Then in five minutes announcing, 'We are going to go to art class soon. Please put your toys away.' When it is time to move on to a new activity, prompting the child by asking, 'What comes next?' and referring him/her to his/her activity schedule can be extremely helpful to the student with Asperger Syndrome. One parent reported that if her child became upset at home with a change in his routine, he would frequently go to his schedule on the refrigerator for reassurance. His mother said that problems would only escalate if the unexpected activity was not on the schedule, and that usually, he was able to calm himself by reviewing the schedule.

Student checklists

Older students may benefit from being able to self-direct their behavior with a checklist. For instance, packing a book bag to go home may seem overwhelming to a child with Asperger Syndrome. The teacher could provide a checklist of the books that he/she needs to take home and give it to the student. The student can then check-off each book as he/she places it in his/her backpack.

XI. USE OF DRAMA AND ROLE-PLAY

Many children with Asperger Syndrome can be taught perspective-taking skills and nonverbal communication skills by being able to take on the role of an actor. Discussing the part that he/she is expected to play, the emotions required, etc., prior to participation in this kind of activity can be useful in helping the student to adopt the part. For instance, demonstrating how the student's face will need to look when the character is sad, angry, or happy can be helpful. In addition, practicing voice inflection and tone will be useful. The student will learn other valuable lessons through drama: the give and take of conversation, the usefulness of gestures in communication, and how emotions can be conveyed through words and nonverbal communication. Drama can be used in some form or another from the preschool years all the way through high school to teach social skills.

Sociodramatic play, or role-playing a social activity in which children relate to one another through roles centered around a theme, is also a useful way to teach appropriate social behavior. For instance, students can role-play in sociodramatic play the parts one would play as a customer who has come to a beauty shop to have his/her hair cut, the stylist, the shampoo person, or the reception-ist. Conversation can be centered around those things that are often discussed in such situations. Students can be provided with minimal props, or they may be given a variety of such items. Re-hearsal of appropriate social communication and behavior through drama can occur after a review of such by the teacher. The teacher can also help by prompting the students with appropriate conver-sation and/or behaviors as the drama progresses. In a study by Howard Goldstein and Connie Cisar at the University of Pitts-burgh (Goldstein and Cisar, 1992) sociodramatic play 'increased the likelihood of variety and creativity during social interactions' (p.279). In addition, 'script training provided a set of common stimuli for all the children. Although children encountered varia-tions in script performance when teamed with new members, the scripts structured the occurrence of discriminative stimuli' (p.279). Because children with Asperger Syndrome and high-functioning autism do best when behaviors can be predicted, sociodramatic play would appear to be helpful to these children. Indeed, many parents of children with Asperger Syndrome rehearse with their children proper ways to begin and maintain conversations with much success.

In summary, a caring teacher who adopts any or all of the above methods of teaching social skills to a child with Asperger Syndrome and/or high-functioning autism will see that he/she

will begin to make meaningful strides in his/her social development. Incorporating social skills instruction that correlates with the
child's method of learning and breaking the social goals into small
concrete tasks are the key components of a successful social skills
curriculum.

CHAPTER SEVEN

IEP Development

(How-To Instructions for Parents)

PREPARING FOR AN EVALUATION

Incorporating social goals into the IEP does not have to be daunting. Adequate information gathering can make the process of identifying and addressing these needs relatively easy. The author recommends following these steps before sitting down to write the IEP.

○ *Gather parent input*

School districts should discuss with the parents problems that they see their child has in the social skills area. They should provide them with a checklist from a social skills assessment so they can rate their child on various skills. Parents have the most opportunity to see him/her in social settings that are less structured. They can see the differences he/she may have as compared to other children of the same age. When questionnaires are sent home to initiate school evaluations, parents need to make sure their comments address the child's needs. For instance, if the questionnaire asks, 'Describe your child,' the parent needs to provide a description of the *problem areas* of the child's *social development.* Too often, parents reply, 'Bright, energetic, blond, blue-eyed.' If the parents feel the questions are not 'teasing' out this appropriate information, they need to turn the form over (with an arrow indicating that they are doing this to the reader) and write, write, write! An attached typed input sheet with their comments is also helpful. Be sure to include things that the child does well (his/her strengths and talents). Also, be sure to include the things that interest and motivate the child – this is information that a teacher would certainly want to know about!

Parent input into comprehensive evaluation reports (CERs) is required by law. CERs drive the IEP. If families feel that their comments or their child's needs are not described adequately, they need to check that they disagree with the CER, add supporting documentation, and request that it be attached to the CER with the notation: 'see addendum.' Signing an IEP that does not address the needs indicated in the CER or in the parents' letter of dissent with a CER is *not recommended.*

o *Use an assessment tool*

As previously discussed in Chapter 5, there exists a variety of social skills assessments that lend well to finding areas of need that the child with Asperger Syndrome may be exhibiting. Get a full picture of the child's social adeptness by not only measuring his/her abilities, but how the *other children* perceive his/her abilities.

o *Observe the child*

Observe the child in a variety of settings, especially in non-structured times (recess, lunch periods, free time) and gather samplings across several days to get an accurate picture of what is going on. Be sure that observations are also done while the child is participating in both small and large groups. The child should not only be observed by his/her teachers, but also people unfamiliar with him/her. For instance, frequently the unbiased perceptions of a recess monitor who sees the child every day may provide more helpful information than individuals more directly involved with his/her school day. Putting the assessment tools aside and just gathering data on the observation itself is also helpful. For instance: 'Today, Joshua seemed agitated. He spent a lot of his recess time pacing back and forth and covering his ears.' A statement such as this may actually help school personnel to focus on *why* Joshua might be agitated.

o *Obtain independent evaluation information*

Parents can enlist a professional trained in autism spectrum disorders to be able to provide his/her expert input. No credentials are required for this type of person and his/her expertise should be accepted as relevant because of his/her extensive background or knowledge in this area. If school districts are not willing to pay for this service, parents should locate such an individual to include his/her opinions in the assessment if it will help school officials create a better program for their child. This may be critical for children whose social problems are not interfering with their academic abilities. Be sure that the report is not more than a year old; otherwise, it may not be considered by the school district as timely.

If you are seeking an independent evaluation report to obtain a particular education program or placement, be sure your evaluator has the right credentials according to your state's laws. For instance, in Pennsylvania, such a person must be a Pennsylvania certified school psychologist. Make sure that these individuals can make educational recommendations and identify areas of need for you, as well as specific ways the district could meet those needs. Independent evaluations must also be considered when districts write their CER reports if the parents request that they be included. Because independent evaluations are so critical to obtaining appropriate services, parents should make an effort to schedule them prior to IEP meetings, particularly as part of CER assessments. Some families schedule one every year so that the input is available and up-to-date.

A word of caution: in preschools, children have the legal right to have all areas of their development addressed if they qualify for an IEP because of a medical diagnosis. Writing IEPs for preschool children that include social skills is, therefore, not difficult. For children with a medical diagnosis who are diagnosed after they have entered elementary school, things get a little trickier. Children with a medical diagnosis also must have a need for specially designed instruction to qualify for an IEP. Specially designed instruction does not have to be just academic instruction. It could include, for instance, social skills instruction, or gross motor skills instruction (typically weak areas in children with Asperger Syndrome). However, in most cases, parents are going to need an independent evaluation detailing these difficulties and specifically listing educational recommendations to qualify. Getting children diagnosed before school age is recommended and having social skills goals on the IEP before transitioning to school age programs begins is very helpful. School districts will see a need for social skills instruction because it is already on their current preschool IEP.

PREPARING FOR AN IEP MEETING

Often parents and educators say that it is extremely difficult to write social goals that are measurable because such skills are not concrete. These arguments can be successfully eliminated if parents and teachers keep in mind the following 'Golden Rules' for developing social IEP goals:

o *Break the social skill problems down into small parts*

Instead of a goal that says, 'Johnny will improve his social skills at recess,' (which would be the equivalent of overhauling all the student's social skills) ask, 'Just what are we trying to get Johnny to do at recess?' As an example, you may find that the following types of goals will come to mind:

1. Johnny will be able to approach a peer and initiate a conversation.

2. Johnny will be able to maintain eye contact in conversation with a peer.

3. Johnny will be able to join in his classmates' games at recess.

4. Johnny will be able to participate in an appropriate conversation with a peer and refrain from talking about trains (or his/her particular pre-occupation).

It is important that the parents and educators pick five or six goals that are the most important to address in the IEP. Writing more than this may become overwhelming for the student. If you examine each of the above, short-term objectives can also be written for each goal. For instance, for the first goal above – 'Johnny will be able to approach a peer and initiate a conversation' – several sub-goals come to mind. Does Johnny understand the proper way to approach a peer? Is he aggressive in his approach or too passive? Does Johnny understand conversation openers? Does

Johnny know how to refrain from talking too much about his obsessions?

The short-term objectives could be written as follows:

1. Johnny will be able to demonstrate the proper way to greet a peer.

2. Johnny will be able to demonstrate the use of appropriate conversation starters with peers.

3. Johnny will be able to refrain from speaking about his obsessions.

4. Johnny will be able to maintain a conversation about a peer's interests.

Goals need to be worded in measurable terms using words such as 'will be able to,' 'will demonstrate,' 'will refrain,' 'will display,' 'will perform.' Here is a list of some other words that could be used to describe social behaviors:

accept	give	permit
allow	greet	praise
compliment	help	react
contribute	interact	respond
cooperate	invite	sit
discuss	join	talk
display	lend	thank
express	make	volunteer

○ *Parents should bring to the IEP meeting any relevant medical diagnosis reports, independent evaluation results and recommendations, as well as last year's IEP*

> They should have all pertinent documents in order and readily accessible. Be sure not to bring *everything* pertaining to your child, just the items that are most recent (less than two years old would be appropriate). Make copies of those that you feel are going to be critical for team members to see before the meeting.

○ *Make a list of all services you think your child will need*

> This list could include speech therapy, help with math or reading, occupational therapy, physical therapy, adaptive physical education, etc. Your independent evaluations should support this need. Again, provide copies for the entire team.
>
> In her book *Creating a Win-Win IEP for Students with Autism*, Beth Fouse (Fouse 1999) provides a wonderful checklist to help parents get ready for an IEP meeting.

FREQUENTLY ASKED PARENT QUESTIONS
What schools and placements are best for children with Asperger Syndrome?

> The author holds to the rule that *there is no particular 'perfect' school or 'placement' for children with Asperger Syndrome!* Many parents ask for the names of schools that provide the best services for children with autism/Asperger Syndrome. Ami Klin, Ph.D., at Yale Child Study at Yale University, states in a teleconference in 1998 that 'a child should have as much integration as he/she can profit from.' The author has worked with hundreds of parents of children with autism and Asperger Syndrome and whole-heartedly agrees with Dr. Klin's observation.

Preparation checklist for the IEP meeting

1. Get and study all relevant information, including:

    A. Assessments for

        (1) Eligibility determination

        (2) Performance levels and progress on goals/objectives

        (3) Related services

    B. Prior IEPs

    C. Teacher progress notes

2. Make a list of your child's present levels of functioning in the following areas:

    A. Academic skills

    B. Developmental skills

    C. Communication, speech, and language development

    D. Physical and motor skills (fine and gross motor)

    E. Emotional/behavioral skills

    F. Social skills/social interaction in school and home environment

    G. Self-help/activities of daily living

    H. Vocational or prevocational skills

3. Make a list of positive outcomes you would like to see for your child.

    A. Develop annual goals from this list.

    B. Ask yourself: Is each outcome or goal realistic?

    C. Ask yourself: Will the goal help my child become more independent?

4. Make a list of special education and related services you believe are necessary for your child to receive educational benefit from special education.

5. Prepare your own information for the IEP meeting.

    A. Document unassessed needs.

        (1) Get letters or reports related to these needs from your child's pediatrician, therapists, and other professionals who know your child.

> (2) Be sure that the letters include a description of your child's special need(s), its educational impact, and a 'prescription' for needed services.
>
> B.   Develop short-term objectives.
>
> 6. Review your child's status. Cooperate with the agency's reasonable evaluation process. Find out if additional testing will be needed to discuss additional services.
>
> 7. Be sure that the IEP committee has accurate reports.
>
> 8. Work things out before the annual review. The best meeting is a short meeting. If you have questions to be resolved or issues of concern, try to work them out prior to the meeting.
>
> 9. If your state allows recording at IEP meetings, take your tape recorder to the meeting. Take several high quality tapes and extra batteries with you.
>
> Beth Fouse, 1999, *Creating a Win-Win IEP for Students with Autism*, Arlington, TX: Future Horizons.

Figure 7.1 Preparation checklist for the IEP meeting

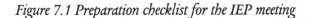

Children cannot learn social skills in a vacuum, and children with Asperger Syndrome are no exception. The ability to observe typical peer interactions, learn the necessary social skills, practice them in small group settings, and generalize them in large group settings can all be accomplished in the regular education environment, provided the student is not a behavior problem and is not having tremendous difficulty academically.

Too often, parents jump on the bandwagon for 'full inclusion' citing the IDEA (Individuals with Disabilities Education Act, 1999): 'Children with disabilities are to be educated in the least restrictive environment.' This mandate is important because it also provides for a rule that stipulates that all the supports a child needs to succeed in the regular education environment need to be provided to encourage placement in the 'least restrictive environment' (LRE). More often than not, this is where school districts and parents hit their brick walls – districts either refuse to provide or cannot afford to provide those supports before the child has demonstrated a need for them (and sometimes even when they have!) and some parents may not be well enough versed in the law to know what those supports are and what their children are entitled to through the IEP process.

Some districts are still in the 'dark ages' with educating special needs children. They have particular elementary classrooms that are designated as 'special needs rooms' or even 'special needs buildings.' When children are transitioning to elementary school, they are sometimes told, 'This building (or this classroom) is where all the children with autism go.' Parents who are not informed about the law may very willingly sign their child up for this placement, not realizing that it will be extremely difficult to remove him/her later. By law, *placements must be based upon the child's needs as set forth in the IEP.* The flip side is also important to look at too: signing a child up for an inclusive placement without the supports he/she needs is like sealing the child's failure in regular education. Sooner or later, his/her behaviors will make it necessary to modify his/her academic schedule, and then eventually he/she will wind up in a specialized classroom, probably with damaged self-esteem and depression as a result of all the trauma he/she had to endure.

As stated before, inclusion is only beneficial if the child is profiting from it. Parents and educators need to look closely at the word 'profit' and weigh the disadvantages with the advantages.

EXAMPLE
'Jason' was mainstreamed with typical children from the age of three. He had average intelligence and displayed some real strengths in mechanical ability and math reasoning. Beginning in first grade, he seemed to be

having a problem not only with social skills, but also with academics. He was slower than the other children in learning to read, his handwriting was poor, and because of his social deficits, he had trouble fitting in with his peers. In second and third grade, he appeared to be really floundering in both reading and math. He was pulled into a learning support class part-time where needed attention was devoted to his sight-word reading and his math computation deficits. There were no social goals in his IEP. The other children began to tease him as his deficits became more noticeable. He had no classroom aide to help him manage his social skills effectively. This resulted in a dramatic increase in behavior problems as Jason inappropriately attempted to respond to the teasing. These increased to the point where he began to get aggressive with his peers. The parents requested a behavior support plan for Jason in third grade, but as of fifth grade, he still did not have one. Jason had difficulty sleeping at night, was explosive at home, suffered from crying jags, practiced self-mutilation, and talked a lot about death. He is now almost a full-time student in learning support class with no opportunities to interact during the school day with typical children because his behaviors will not permit it. He is also on very strong doses of an anti-depressant.

Sadly, Jason's story is not unusual. A child with Asperger Syndrome who is placed in the regular education environment *without supports* will almost always have difficulty with either academic or social skills, sometimes both. A child who is taking medication for depression or anxiety due to school-related problems should be immediately 'red-flagged' to determine what modifications need to be made to eliminate the stress, reduce the anxiety, and help with self-esteem. He/she may not be in the best placement after all. Advocates for inclusion need to consider whether the idea of full inclusion is worth the trade-off of the student's mental health. Educators and parents should really listen to the child, learn what his/her problem areas are, and address them as a team. Oftentimes, a supportive teacher, willing to go the extra mile, can really pull it all together for the student. Parents need to look at this as well when considering placements!

The main purpose of having a child with autism (or any other child with a disability for that matter) included in regular education is to help him/her learn to use appropriate social skills and to model from typical peers. The individual with Asperger Syndrome will not have opportunities to practice social skills if he/she does not have interactions with typically developing children. Many parents of children with high-functioning autism think that this shouldn't be a prime consideration for the early preschool years when considering the types of available treatment programs for their children. This author would like to emphasize that failing to provide these opportunities can certainly have a detrimental affect on their future social development. As we have seen in Chapter 4, even very young children are developing social awareness and learning acceptable social behavior from their peers. Failing to provide such opportunities to develop social skills is not a recommended practice for children with Asperger Syndrome.

When the child reaches school-age, some districts will offer an autism support classroom to accommodate the needs of the child with Asperger Syndrome. When parents observe the class, they may decide this placement is good for him/her. Others may observe the class and feel that their child is 'too advanced' for this placement, even though the teacher has been trained in their child's disability. Some districts offer an emotional support class where children can receive their social skills instruction, and this could be quite beneficial for some children. In other schools, a learning support classroom is used to accommodate these needs. For some parents, a regular education classroom will be appropriate. Technically, the IEP should be written *first* before choosing a placement. The IEP drives the placement, not the other way around. Parents should *always* have an opportunity to choose the least restrictive placement first with supports. For some, a learning support class (or one of the others above) may end up being the least restrictive placement for their child. This is quite feasible as long as this is a team decision and options were made available to the parents, including the option of regular education with supports.

How can I write accountability into the IEP?

Parents frequently ask, 'What if my child just isn't meeting the IEP goals? Is the district liable?' The answer is, 'No,' unless your district is simply not addressing them. The IEP is a service contract, not a performance contract. However, IEP goals that are continually not met, year after year, need to be re-evaluated. Are these goals really attainable? (Experts will offer insight as to this.) Are the goals measurable?

Ms. Rebecca Volaire, educational advocate for the Mental Health Association in Westmoreland County, Greensburg, Pennsylvania, says that parents should make sure that there are benchmarks included in the IEP – statements that indicate where the child is functioning *before* the IEP goal is implemented. Throughout the school year, data should be kept on goal progress to determine if the child is improving his/her benchmarks.

One parent was not satisfied sending her child to school not knowing what was going on with her child's IEP. Yes, the autistic support teacher was pulling her child out once a week to address these needs; yes, this teacher was reporting back to her on what she did; but how did the parent know if the child was improving? Here are some ways to build accountability.

○ *Checklists and report forms*

Design a checklist that lists the IEP goals. Have the IEP team dis-
tribute these checklists and report forms to teachers and individuals
in the mainstream who have opportunities to work with the child
with Asperger Syndrome. Valuable insight can be achieved this
way.

IEP Goals		
Date_____		
	YES	NO
1. Eye contact while interacting with peers		
2. Eye contact while interacting with adults		
3. Responds appropriately to peer touch		
4. Gives and accepts compliments		
5. Offers assistance to peers		

Figure 7.2 IEP Goals

○ *Parent observation*

Parents should also observe at least once every nine weeks to see
how the child is progressing. Team meetings can then be held to
modify or change the IEP as necessary. Your IEP is a fluid
document – you can update it at any time!

○ *Student self-evaluation forms*

The student with Asperger Syndrome can also share what he/she
feels are his/her problem areas. Be sure to include statements where
the student can evaluate what he/she sees as a strength in a particular area as well! Self-esteem can be a good indicator of how things
are going in the classroom and can be monitored this way.

Social Skills Observation Checkpoint

Date: _____

IEP goal	Place observed (recess, lunch, etc.)	Yes/No
Initiated conversation with a peer		
Approached a peer to join in play		
Maintained eye contact with peers		
Maintained the topic of conversation in three exchanges with a peer		

Figure 7.3 Social skills observation checkpoint

o *Social skills report cards*

A report on your child's progress should be provided to you as often as the regular education children receive report cards. This is the law. The law does not stipulate how this report card must be designed, so parents should design their own to get maximum information on their child's progress and request the team to adopt it.

Physical Education Self-Evaluation Form

Today's Date _____

What activities did you enjoy most about this week's gym class?

_____

_____

What activities do you feel that you were particularly good at in this week's gym class?

_____

_____

What activities do you feel you need to improve in gym class?

_____

_____

Additional Comments:

_____

_____

Figure 7.4 Physical education self-evaluation form

o *Lesson summary reports*

Lesson summary reports can be designed by the team to communicate to you how each social skills lesson worked for your child. For instance, if your child is pulled out with typical children for a social skills lesson, the lesson summary report is a form of communication sent home to you about how the goal was addressed, how the child practiced it, and how he/she performed and demonstrated under-

---

Social Skills Report Card

Name of student _____   Date _____

Key:

Mastered   1

Good   2

Average   3

Poor   4

Goals:		1	2	3	4
1.	Responds appropriately to teasing.	___	___	___	___
2.	Uses self-control and self-calming techniques.	___	___	___	___
3.	Uses tact with peers and adults.				
4.	Offers assistance to peers.				

Comments:

Figure 7.5 Social skills report card

standing of this goal. One popular version of this is through a communications notebook. However, the student may object to this practice and consider it an embarrassment. A recommendation might be a dated lesson summary, handwritten or typed after the class, that is placed in a sealed envelope and sent home in the child's book-bag. Keep in mind, this may be unrealistic for a teacher with several students. Having the child's personal assistant complete this task or using a checklist (above) might be more reasonable.

Note: Pay close attention to the 'Methods of Evaluation' section of your child's IEP. By listing the teacher checklists, the student self-evaluation forms, and social skills report cards in the IEP and attaching copies of these actual forms to your IEP, you are requiring the district to use them.

What is the 'specially designed instruction' section of my IEP? What is it used for?

The specially designed instruction section of your IEP is where modifications to the classroom and the use of special techniques can be written from Chapter 6. This section is where the issue of how the goals are going to be implemented is addressed. For instance, here are some specially designed instruction techniques that were written into the IEP of an eight-year-old student with Asperger Syndrome:

- Use of Carol Gray's social stories.

- Use of Skill-Streaming Curriculum.

- Use of small group instruction with typical peers.

- Use of visual strategies such as comic strips and schedules.

There is currently a concern that schools need to avoid listing particular curriculums on the IEP. If the curriculum is not taught in the manner prescribed by the author of the text, the district may be held liable in due process. For example, one parent recently stressed that Carol Gray's social stories was an excellent way for her son to learn social skills. The IEP team agreed and wrote it in her IEP. The teacher, however, was not trained in the particular 'formula' of writing Carol Gray's stories and invented her own method. The parents felt that Carol Gray's method was more effective and filed a complaint with the Department of Education in Pennsylvania, citing noncompliance. The district was advised to refrain from writing specific curriculums in the IEP as a protective measure to them in the future. Some districts are still willing to include such curriculums as 'specially designed instruction' because they recognize the validity of research on particular curriculums written for children with Asperger Syndrome. They agree to use it because they want to address the child's needs in the most appropriate manner. If curriculums exist that do the job, then by all means, use them! It is also important that parents maintain an 'open-mindedness' about input that teachers may have about methods that they have used in the classroom that they would like to include in the IEP. Your child's teacher may not be well known in the field of autism, but he/she may have worked with another child that responded well to their proposed instruction. As Rebecca Volaire states, 'You can't build attitude into the IEP.' Parents should do everything possible to preserve a good working relationship with their child's teachers so that they do not feel as if working with your child is too much of a burden. The other side of the coin applies too; teachers need to make sure that parents are consulted for their input. In their search to help their child, many parents have become very informed about the methods and treatments currently available. They also know their child the best.

If the 'specially designed instruction' section of the IEP does not list pullout sessions with typical peers (small group instruction), one can assume that all the learning will take place in the regular education classroom. Parents will need to be extra vigilant that regular education teachers across all domains are providing documentation that the goal is being taught and being reinforced in a way that will be effective for the child. For instance, if a child has a social goal that reads, 'Johnny will be able to display appropriate eye contact' and the only one who asks him to do this is his classroom teacher, Johnny will learn that it is not necessary to display eye contact with his other teachers.

What is the related services portion of my IEP used for?

IDEA defines related services as 'transportation and such developmental, corrective, and other supportive services as are required to assist a child with a disability to benefit from special education.' Related services are used to maintain a student's placement in the *least restrictive environment* and must be related to their disability. These types of services may include:

- speech therapy

- physical therapy

- occupational therapy

- counseling services

- school health services

- social work services in schools.

The list is not complete and may include other supportive services (including, for instance, art or music therapy) if they are required to assist a child with a disability to benefit from special education.

However, they must be based on assessments, be able to be performed during school hours, and stated in the IEP with duration, time, and frequency.

Therapy can take place as 'direct therapy' (a service provider works directly with a student to achieve IEP goals), or 'consultative therapy' (where a service provider can help other professionals achieve the student's IEP goals). Consultative services may actually result in more individual time for the student than direct therapy because of the need to observe, interact, and provide feedback and suggestions to his/her teachers. Progress reports for consultative therapy should be reported to parents as frequently as for direct therapy. Logs should be kept that verify the duration, time, and frequency that the service was provided so that there is no question as to whether those amounts match the duration, time, and frequency amounts detailed in the IEP.

What can the IEP team do if the teachers that work with our child are not trained in Asperger Syndrome, and yet are critical to the success of our child's program?

The key here is what do you mean *specifically* with regards to training? If you are not specific, then requesting an 'autism' training may not be sufficient for your child with 'Asperger Syndrome.' As an example, one parent secured a teacher training in Asperger Syndrome for her child's IEP, but the principal only included the primary classroom teacher in the training and not the other teachers or the classroom aide that frequently interacted with the child. If the team agrees that teacher training is necessary, it can be written in the 'supports for parents and personnel' section of the IEP. Parents should also be invited to participate in the training as team members and to offer their comments. A request for instructors to read applicable literature regarding your child's disability can also be written into the IEP.

Many parents provide their new teachers with a small amount of reading material explaining the child's diagnosis, what deficits and strengths he/she has as a result of this disability, and what has worked for him/her. This can also be written as 'parent-provided training materials' in the IEP. However, many schools require that the principal or special education director must approve the materials first.

Parents themselves may feel that they also need additional services to enable them to become more effective team members. Parents may want to pursue attending IEP development courses or learn more about their child's disability as he/she participates in regular education. Reimbursement for such training could also be written and included in this section of the IEP.

My child seems to lose all the social skills he has developed over long breaks and after summer vacation. Is there anything I can do about this?

Every IEP team must make an annual determination of whether a child needs extended school year (ESY) services or not, to prevent him/her from losing the skills he/she has worked so hard to attain during the school year. Parents should have the opportunity to provide input as to why this service is necessary. Typically, school districts may claim that extended school year services are for children who suffer *academic* regression. The law varies from state to state with regards to this, and you should become aware of what services can be provided in your own state under ESY and not take this statement for granted. The author has seen many social skills programs implemented under ESY.

In conclusion, keep in mind these helpful rules for developing an IEP:

1. The IEP is a powerful tool to achieve what you want for your child in social skills instruction. The law requires you to have input into its development.

2. Be especially aware if your IEP looks the same as every other child's IEP. The IEP is an *individualized* education plan.

3. Parents should be well-trained in the use of different parts of the IEP.

4. Parents should be able to write meaningful and measurable goals for social skills instruction.

5. Parents should come to the IEP meeting with a plan for what they see as their child's greatest needs in this area.

6. The district should be able to provide to the parent evidence of progress towards the goals once the plan has been implemented.

7. If the plan is not working, parents should immediately re-open the IEP.

8. Above all, parents should understand that the process of developing an IEP is not about 'winning' what *they* want for their child with Asperger Syndrome. It's also not about what *the district* is willing to provide for this student. The IEP is a written summary of what the *team* together feels is appropriate and necessary to provide the child with Asperger Syndrome a meaningful education that meets his/her individual needs.

Incorporating social goals into the IEP for children with high-functioning autism and Asperger Syndrome and diligently working to achieve these goals will provide children with this diagnosis with the tools to navigate a pathway toward a bright and productive future.

References

American Psychiatric Association (1994) *Diagnostic and Statistical Manual of Mental Disorders*, 4th edn. Washington, DC: American Psychiatric Association.

Asperger, H. (1944) 'Die Autistischen Psychopathen.' *Kindesalter, Archiv. fur Psychiatrie und Nervenkrankheiten 117*, 76–136.

Attwood, T. (1998) *Asperger's Syndrome: A Guide for Parents and Professionals*. London: Jessica Kingsley Publishers.

Baker, M., Koegel, R. and Koegel, L. (1998) 'Increasing the Social Behavior of Young Children with Autism Using Their Obsessive Behaviors.' *Journal of the Association for Persons with Severe Handicaps, 23, 4*, 300–308.

Bierman, K., Smoot, D. and Aumiller, K. (1993) 'Characteristics of Aggressive-Rejected, Aggressive (Nonrejected), and Rejected (Non-Aggressive) Boys.' *Child Development 64*, 139–151.

Charlop, M. and Milstein, J. (1989) 'Teaching Autistic Children Conversational Speech Using Video Modeling.' *Journal of Applied Behavior Analysis 3*, 275–285.

Charlop-Christy, M. and Haymes, L. (1996) 'Using Obsessions as Reinforcers With and Without Mild Reductive Procedures to Decrease Inappropriate Behaviors of Children with Autism.' *Journal of Autism and Developmental Disorders 26, 5*, 527–545.

Coie, J. (1990) 'Toward a Theory of Peer Rejection.' In S. R. Asher and J. D. Coie (eds) *Peer Rejection in Childhood*. Cambridge: Cambridge University Press.

Coie, J. and Dodge, K. (1983) 'Continuities and Changes in Children's Social Status: A Five-Year Longitudinal Study.' *Merrill-Palmer Quarterly 29*, 261–282.

Coie, J., Dodge, K. and Coppotelli, H. (1982) 'Dimensions and Types of Status: A Cross-Age Perspective.' *Developmental Psychology 18*, 557–570.

Coie, J., Dodge, K. and Kupersmidt, J. B. (1990) 'Peer Group Behavior and Social Status.' In S. R. Asher and J. D. Coie (eds) *Peer Rejection in Childhood*. Cambridge: Cambridge University Press.

Cumine, V., Leach, J. and Stevenson, G. (1998) *Asperger Syndrome: A Practical Guide for Teachers*. London: David Fulton Publishers.

Forest, M., Falvey, M., Rosenberg, R. and Pearpoint, J. (1993 revised) *All My Life is a Circle.* Toronto, Canada: Inclusion Press.

Fouse, B. (1999) *Creating a Win-Win IEP for Students with Autism.* Arlington, TX: Future Horizons.

Fouse, B. and Wheeler, M. (2000) *A Treasure Chest of Behavioral Strategies for Individuals with Autism.* Arlington, TX: Future Horizons.

Gesell, A. and Ilg, F. (1946) *The Child from Five to Ten.* New York: Harper and Row Publishers.

Goldstein, H. and Cisar, C. (1992) 'Promoting Interaction During Sociodramatic Play: Teaching Scripts to Typical Preschoolers and Classmates with Disabilities.' *Journal of Applied Behavior Analysis 25*, 2, 265–280.

Grandin, T. (1995) *Thinking in Pictures and Other Reports from my Life with Autism.* New York: Doubleday Publishers.

Gray, C. (1994) *Comic Strip Conversations.* Arlington, TX: Future Horizons.

Gray, C. (1994) *The Original Social Story Book.* Arlington, TX: Future Horizons.

Handlan, S. and Bloom, L. (1993) 'The Effect of Educational Curricula and Modeling/ Coaching on the Interactions of Kindergarten Children with their Peers with Autism.' *Focus on Autistic Behavior 8*, 2, 1–11.

Hodgon, L. (1998) *Visual Strategies.* Troy, Michigan: Quirk-Roberts Publishing. (1999) *Individuals with Disabilities Education Act (IDEA).* Published at 20 U.S. C. Sections 1400, et. seq., and the implementing regulations published at 34 C.F. R. Part 300.

KidAccess, Inc., Product Line: 'Eye-cons' Visual Supports. 6526 Darlington Road, Pittsburgh, PA 15217.

Klin, Ami. (1998) 'Asperger's Syndrome: Implications for Education.' 1998–1999 Autism Teleconference Series, Central Instructional Support Center, Pennsylvania Department of Education and Pennsylvania Department of Welfare.

McAllister, J., Moyes, R., Preator, K. and Bagnato, S. (1996) *Valuing Diversity in Young Children with Autism: Recognizing and Developing Strengths.* (Unpublished)

McClannahan, L. (1999) *Activity Schedules for Children with Autism.* Bethesda, MD.: Woodbine House.

McGinnis, E. and Goldstein, A. (1997) *Skillstreaming the Elementary School Child.* Illinois: Research Press.

Minshew, N. (1988) 'New Perspectives in Autism, Part I: The Clinical Spectrum of Autism.' *Current Problems in Pediatrics 18*, 561–610.

O'Connell, T. (1974) 'The Musical Life of an Autistic Boy.' *Journal of Autism and Childhood Schizophrenia 4*, 223–229.

Parten, M. (1932) 'Social Play Among Preschool Children.' In R.E.H. and B. Sutton-Smith (eds) *Child's Play*. New York: Wiley.

Prizant, B. M. (1987) 'Clinical Implications of Echolalic Behavior in Autism.' In T. Layton (ed) *Language and Treatment of Autistic and Developmentally Disordered Children*. Illinois: Charles Thomas.

Prizant, B. M. and Duchan, J. F. (1981) 'The Functions of Immediate Echolalia in Autistic Children.' *Journal of Speech and Hearing Disorders 46*, 241–249.

Quill, K. (1995) *Teaching Children with Autism – Strategies to Enhance Communication and Socialization*. New York: Delmar Publishers. (1973) *Rehabilitation Act, Section 504*. Published at 29 U.S. C. Section 794 and the implementing regulations published at 34 C. F. R. Part 104.

Rubin, K. and Stewart, S. (1996) 'Social Withdraw.' In E. J. Marsh and R. A. Barkley (eds) *Child Psychopathology*. New York: Guilford Press.

Walker, H. M. and McConnell, S. (1988) 'Scale of Social Competence and School Adjustment.' In the *Walker Social Skills Curriculum: The Accepts Program*. Texas: Pro-Ed.

Willey, L. (1999) *Pretending to be Normal*. London: Jessica Kingsley Publishers.

Williams, D. (1992) *Nobody Nowhere. The Extraordinary Autobiography of an Autistic*. New York: Times Books.

Subject Index

Name Index